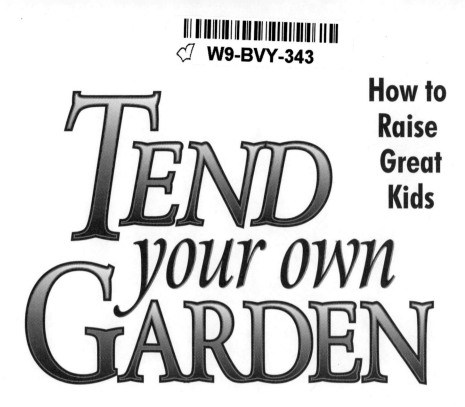

TEND *your own* GARDEN

How to Raise Great Kids

TEND your own GARDEN

How to Raise Great Kids

Timothy E. O'Connell, Ph.D.

Foreword by Mitch and Kathy Finley

ThomasMore®
– An RCL Company –

Allen, Texas

Cover Design by Melody Loggins, Zia Designs
Book Interior Design by Bernadette Reyna, Zia Designs

Author photo on back cover by Pete Stenberg

ACKNOWLEDGMENTS
The publisher gratefully acknowledges permission to reprint the following material:
Make Our Garden Grow. Music by Leonard Bernstein and Lyrics by Richard
Wilbur, copyright 1955, 1958, 1974, 1982, 1990, 1994 by The Estate of Leonard
Bernstein. Copyright renewed. Leonard Bernstein Music Publishing Company
LLC, Publisher. Reprinted by permission of Boosey & Hawkes, Inc., sole agent.

Send all inquiries to:

Thomas More®
An RCL Company
200 East Bethany Drive
Allen, Texas 75002-3804

Toll Free: 800-264-0368
Fax: 800-688-8356
Visit our website at www.rclweb.com

Printed in the United States of America

Library of Congress Catalog Card Number 98-60970
ISBN 0-88347-417-4
7417

1 2 3 4 5   03 02 01 00 99

To
D & B
G & J

Raising Great Kids!

ACKNOWLEDGMENTS

The learning that undergirds this book has taken place over decades. So it's impossible to name all the influences that have aided me. In fact, just about anyone who's crossed my path through the years can take some credit for these thoughts. Still, I am particularly aware of how much I have learned from the students who have taken my classes, participants in my workshops, and clients who have allowed me to share in the journeys of their lives.

You will not be surprised to learn that I am especially grateful to those whose experiences provide the basis for the many stories in this book. At the same time, you should know that I have consistently changed details in the stories to protect confidentiality. I have also modified some stories both to further disguise them and for narrative focus.

In the completion of the manuscript I was the beneficiary of wonderful suggestions from Nancy Schiller, who read the manuscript with care and insight, and from Mary Kaye Cisek, with whom I discussed many of the ideas. And most especially, I was blessed with the suggestions of Larry Little, my most consistent and supportive critic.

Finally, my publishing colleagues at Thomas More Publishing and RCL Enterprises managed the delicate deed of asking the right questions while remaining encouraging, of moving things along smartly while assuring that things were done right. My special thanks to Bill Huebsch, who first proposed this project, to John Sprague, my publisher, and to Debra Hampton, my extraordinary editor. It continues to be a delight to work with these folks.

TABLE OF CONTENTS

FOREWORD

by Mitch and Kathy Finley

Mitch and Kathy Finley, internationally known speakers on family life, are the parents of three sons. They are the authors of Building Christian Families *(Thomas More, 1996).*

Most playgrounds, in years gone by, included a piece of recreational equipment called a teeter-totter, a long board or pole with seats on both ends, balanced across a sturdy fulcrum of some sort. The idea was for one kid to sit on each end of the teeter-totter. When one kid was up, the other kid was down—up and down, up and down the two kids would go. It could be an exhilarating lot of fun. Of course, if one kid was heavier than the other, he or she could keep the other kid up in the air indefinitely. Or, the kid who was down could suddenly jump off the seat, allowing the kid who was up to crash to the ground and see stars.

Ah, me. When was the last time you saw a teeter-totter in a public playground? If casual observation serves, it appears that the teeter-totter is fast disappearing. Probably the committees convened to oversee the building of playgrounds these days judge the teeter-totter too dangerous. All the same, the teeter-totter is a good metaphor for the experience of parents in today's world.

Parenting is a balancing act in more ways than one. Moms and dads must be concerned constantly with raising a good, healthy human being. Trouble is, babies do not come with instructions included, and every last one of them is unique. Just when you think you have the child figured out you find yourself surprised, astonished, or aghast. Just when you learn to cope with or tolerate the "terrible twos," the offspring moves into the "fantastic fours." When it is clear to all that your teenager is a lost cause, he or she with no advance warning exhibits responsible behavior!

To be a father or mother is to experience a great many ups and downs, and just when you are up you may find yourself down. Or vice-versa. There are times when parents are down, and suddenly the beaming smile of a baby or a teenager's suddenly articulated wisdom can send you sky-high with joy. In all these situations, however, Timothy O'Connell's central insight is right on the money.

What matters most, if you would be "a good parent" is not your knowledge of "parenting skills"—immensely valuable as such skills can be—but who you are as a person, your level of maturity, the values and goals that are important to you, the religious and philosophical beliefs that you live daily. O'Connell's advice to "tend your own garden" is, therefore, the best advice any parent will ever receive, because what children need more than anything is parents who are grown-ups.

Years ago, Sidney Cornelia Callahan wrote a book we read when our three sons were two, and five, and seven. That book, *Parenting: Principles and Politics of Parenthood* (Doubleday, 1973), includes a chapter titled "What Does a Good Parent Do?" and in that chapter Callahan wrote: "An essential goal of human parenthood is. . .to make our children glad they were born and eager for life."

Keeping to Timothy O'Connell's theme, parents who would strive for this goal must ask themselves, "Am I glad I was born and eager for life?" The response we give to this very personal question may surface all kinds of things to think about and tend to—not in our children but in ourselves. "Physician, heal thyself," goes the ancient adage, and we may translate it thus: "Parents, grow up yourselves." For it is only parents who are adults who can hope to raise children who will become mature adults in their own good time.

Someone once articulated a poetic insight for parents that became worn and weary from overuse, yet its value remains undiminished for all that. It goes like this: "The main task of parents is to give their children roots and wings." If we keep this book's central theme in mind, if we as parents "tend our own garden" as the basic task of parenthood, then we will remain focused on this goal, to give our children roots in what is life-giving and strong wings to fly away into lives and identities of their own.

In order to do this, of course, we must live with the possibility that our children may become people we never intended or could have predicted. Regardless of how grown-up we are, no matter how good and effective we are as parents, in the long run our children are God's children and not our own. Sometimes, in other words, one of the most difficult challenges for parents is to trust in God's love for their children. To say this is one thing, to act on it quite another.

In the long run our children leave us to become their own unique selves, and—unless we "luck out" and have nearly perfect children—sometimes that includes embracing values we may not like, making mistakes with painful consequences, even becoming people who, to all appearances, are not glad they were born and are not eager for life. All we can do as parents is all we can do, and then all we can do is stand back and see what happens. We may be pleased with the results, we may not be pleased, or we may have mixed feelings. Regardless, our children are in God's hands, and what better hands could they be in?

Patience is absolutely necessary. As one grandmother told a group of young parents, "You don't know how your kids will turn out until they're forty years old, so you might as well relax and just keep on praying for them."

In the end, the words of Timothy O'Connell shine like the sun, and we do well to make them our own: "How can we succeed in transmitting our values to our children? Or at the very least, how can we increase the likelihood that our children will embrace the values that are ours?" This book will answer those questions. And what is that answer? "Tend your own garden!"

Let the gardening begin. . .

This One's For You

There I was, sitting in the diner. I didn't really need lunch, I wasn't really hungry. It was just that I needed to get out of the house. I was struggling to find a way to begin this conversation, this set of reflections that you now hold in your hands. But, while I knew, in general, what I wanted to share with you, I just couldn't find a way to begin. Despite my best efforts, nothing was coming.

So I decided to buy myself some time by going out for a corned beef sandwich!

I sat there, scribbling notes, playing with alternatives. But still nothing came clear. And then I looked up. And there, across the tables of that simple eatery, I saw him, sitting in the small booth in the corner.

He was a middle-aged man, an African American dressed in rough clothes with an old baseball cap on top of his head. He had the weathered face of one who works outside, earning his bread in the heat and the cold. He was eating lunch. But mostly he was tending his daughter. She was firmly seated in her high-chair, safe and secure. And she was very happy. She ate a bit of food, and then dropped a bit onto the floor. She watched it fall, giggling at the silliness of it all. She took up her little stuffed doll, held it, pulled on it, and then dropped it off the side and watched it sail to the floor.

Such a wonderful time she was having. And such a wonderful time he was having! I watched that man, and in a flash I realized where I should begin.

This book is for that man, and for the love he bears his daughter.

This man is not alone, of course. Just yesterday I was on an airplane from Atlanta to Chicago. Moments before the plane was to depart, a harried mother boarded, holding a diaper bag in one hand, and a small girl, perhaps six months old, in the other. The mother set about removing her coat while continuing to hold the baby. I don't think she ever would have succeeded, except (and here is the wonder of it) several people immediately reached up to help her. One woman took the bag from her hand; a man helped the mother out of her coat. And when she was settled in her seat, several nearby passengers helped to stow her gear.

And last week I shared dinner with a couple, long-time friends, and their four-year-old son. The love lavished on that son was obvious, and I was drawn into it, smiling at his comments, responding seriously to his endless questions, congratulating him on finishing his dinner, and helping him get settled in front of the TV (thank God for the Disney channel!) while we finished ours.

In all these cases, my observation was the same: Nothing is more important to parents than their children.

I'll bet the same is true with you. Very likely you are a parent, and you worry about your children. You love them and protect them, you teach them and advise them. And nothing is as important as they are.

Tend Your Own Garden

Even if you are not a parent, surely there are little people some-where who call forth your care and concern. They may be young rel-atives, or the children of friends. They may be children who are abandoned by those who should care for them, refugees and orphans and victims. In any case, they are the sweet breath of the future. And our hearts dream of helping them find a space where they can truly, fully live.

∞

But what do the children need? Children need many things.

The basic life necessities, of course. It doesn't do much good to provide high-level education to children who are starving. Indeed, as any teacher will tell you, students who are hungry can't concentrate on the lessons anyway. So first of all, the children we love need food and drink, heat and clothes.

And maybe even more basically, children need safety. Recently there was an item on the news about children caught in the crossfire of gang violence. The report explained that a particular school was suffering from high absenteeism. The reason, it turned out, was that the chil-dren were so disturbed by the gunfire they heard that they were afraid to leave their homes and walk to school. It was just too unsafe.

The beautiful end of the story is that a group of fathers banded together to escort the children. They went to the apartment of each child, introduced themselves to the mom and the child, walked with the child the whole way to the school, and finally passed the child into the hands of the teacher. Now, that's an example of adults seeing to the safety of children! And heaven knows children need safety.

But they need other things as well. Children need education. I will never forget a powerful scene in the movie about the life of Helen Keller, who was born blind and deaf. Her teacher, Annie Sullivan struggles to find a way to get through to Helen. Over and over, Annie tries to communicate with Helen, tapping on her wrist in the coded patterns of sign language. But nothing works.

Then, in a stroke of genius, Annie drags Helen to the faucet, forces her hand under the spigot and taps out, over and over, the letters W-A-T-E-R. Suddenly a glimmer of recognition flashes across Helen's face. She pauses; you can almost see the wheels turning inside her head. And then she moves. She taps the letters in return. The concept, the idea, suddenly comes alive for her. In one of those leaps that mark the development of the human person, she realizes: THIS means THAT! And with that moment of education, Helen's future becomes for the first time truly possible.

So it is with all our children, even if the process is a good bit less dramatic. It is only with education that they are able to become adults, in the best, fullest sense of that word. Sure, they can grow bigger; they can add pounds and inches. But physical size doesn't make an adult, personal fullness does. And that fullness cannot happen without education.

∞

Education, and one thing more. What our children need is values. They need morals. They need a sense of right and wrong. They need a sense of what's important in life, and why. They need a sense of values.

Oh, I know that a "sense of values" doesn't sound as obvious as food and drink. But ask any parent: What do you want for your child? The answer you'll hear will not only wish a life for the child. It will also wish a particular way of living. If I could have talked with that wonderful man who sat across the room in the diner feeding his little daughter, I have no doubt about what I would have heard. "I want her to grow up safe and healthy," he would have said. "I want her to be happy. I want her to be able to follow her dreams and achieve her goals." But sooner or later, he would have added: "I want her to be a good person, to tell the truth and keep her promises, to be caring and compassionate, to give love as well as receive it. Yes, I want her to be happy, and I want her to be good."

And so do we all.

It's not easy, passing along our values. Passing along our genes: now that's easy. Without even trying, our children end up looking like us. They get their mother's hair and their father's eyes. The children's height, their complexion, even their temperament may be easy to predict. Passing along these qualities is a simple matter of chromosomes. But not so with our values. Passing on our values is a whole lot more complicated.

But it's just as important. We want our children to be happy, sure. But we also have some convictions about what makes people happy. We don't think happiness is just an accident, or that it can be achieved willy-nilly. There is a particular path to happiness, and one must follow the way. So in wishing our children happiness, we are also wishing them these convictions, we are wishing them the way that we believe in. These values, these ideas about what is really important in life: this, too, is an important part of what we want to pass on to our children.

How is that done? How can we succeed in transmitting our values to our children? Or at the very least, how can we increase the likelihood that our children will embrace the values that are ours? This book will answer those questions. And what is that answer? Tend your own garden!

For over fifteen years I have been studying this issue, and in this book I will tell you what I've learned. I will not just offer my personal opinions; that would be too undependable. Who knows if my experience is right? Who knows if it would apply to others as well? No, I will tell you what I've learned. And what have I learned? Tend your own garden!

For fifteen years, and more, I have been observing all sorts of parents, and I have watched as their children grew older. For fifteen years I have been talking to others who, in turn, have been studying people who are trying to pass along their values. For fifteen years I have been reading the conclusions of scholars who have studied this process, and I have tested their conclusions against the experiences of those I've observed. And what have I found? Tend your own garden!

Some of the ideas may not surprise you. After all, you have been living all your life in the garden of human values. You have seen the most beautiful of flowers bloom, and you have observed the horrible intrusion of weeds. You yourself were raised by people who wanted to pass their values along to you. You, in turn, have been trying to pass along your values to your children. And you, too, have been watching those around you, to see how it was done to them and how they are doing it.

Tend Your Own Garden

So you're not exactly new to this question. Nor will you be completely surprised by the answers. The challenges of tending your garden will not feel altogether new. But if some of the insights are not surprising, they should still be helpful. For they will say clearly and boldly what you might now only suspect to be the case.

But some of the ideas will surprise you greatly. At least, they surprised me. Sometimes the truths of this garden proved to be quite other than I would have guessed. Some acts of tending that struck me as very important turned out not to be important, at all. And some interventions that I had never considered proved to be critical. So I was genuinely surprised.

The same thing may happen to you. Hearing these ideas, the new and surprising ideas, spoken clearly and boldly will challenge you, make you think again about your experience. And it may lead you to change a few things, to modify the way you work in trying to pass along the values you deeply cherish. It may lead you to view in a new way the challenge to tend your garden.

In any case, these ideas will help you. You do, after all, want to pass along those values. Like that wonderful man in the diner, you have a gift you want to present to your children. It's a valuable gift, a gift you hope they will receive and cherish and use. It's a gift that may be the key to a truly successful life for them. Like that man, you want to give your children what they need. And among the things they need, they surely need values by which to live. So you want to present that gift, as well. And these ideas will help you do that.

Yes, this one's for the man in the diner, and for his daughter.

And this one's for you!

Questions to Ponder...

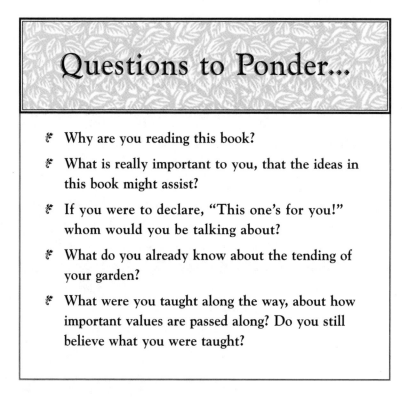

❧ Why are you reading this book?

❧ What is really important to you, that the ideas in this book might assist?

❧ If you were to declare, "This one's for you!" whom would you be talking about?

❧ What do you already know about the tending of your garden?

❧ What were you taught along the way, about how important values are passed along? Do you still believe what you were taught?

2

Been Different Places

I sat there quietly, trying to mind my tongue. We were in the family room, a comfortable space with chairs surrounding a big television. These people are my friends, I kept saying to myself. So I shouldn't be as angry as I am.

But I was angry. Here we were, supposedly sharing a television event. Indeed, it was a public event, the convention of a major political party, a time for proclaiming the values of the party, for selecting the leaders for the future, for presenting the candidates in the upcoming election. This should be a time of pride, I would think, a time for relishing the wonderful traditions of our country. But instead, the speaker whose face filled the screen was indulging in the worst kind of demagoguery. He was being sarcastic, even nasty. He was mocking those who disagreed with him. To his mind, they were not just wrong, they were fools. With his substantial skill he was inviting his audience to taste blood-lust and disdain.

And my fellow viewers, these friends of mine, were loving it. I felt like I was in the grandstand at the Coliseum (the one in Rome, that is), and my friends were cheering the victory of the lions over the

Christians. There was a glee in their responses to the malicious one-liners of the speaker, a delight at his put-downs. In it all there was a meanness, a cold and callous spirit. I don't know if my response was more sadness or genuine fury.

How could this be? How could these friends of mine, people I knew and loved, be so easily buying into this ugliness? And to be fair in the asking of my questions, how could it be that what struck them as merely humorous struck me as so offensive? How was it that I was so disturbed by what they saw as merely entertaining?

I must confess that I did not ask these questions as I sat in front of the television. No, I just did my best to keep my mouth shut! But later, much later, I did ask those questions. And they are important questions for us.

We live in a world of frightening diversity. Think of any attitude, any conviction, any point of view—and I can find you someone who holds it! The daytime talk shows make a fortune entertaining us with people who hold the most outrageous positions. It's enough to make you think that nothing is for sure.

I live in a city, and part of this way of life is riding public transportation. I mount the bus or slide onto the train, and I enter a world of astonishing diversity. The people I see come in all sizes, of course, and colors. Their ages range from beginning to end. But the diversity that really strikes me is the diversity of their ideas. I hear them talking to their friends, and they talk with amazing candor. I learn how much people earn, and what they spend their money on. It isn't what I spend mine on! I learn their sexual practices, and the standards that guide them. I learn what they like to eat, where they like to play, and how they like to live. And what I hear is so different, so astonishingly different, from what is true for me.

There is so much diversity. And you don't need to ride the big-city train with me to see it. You see it in your hometown, no matter how small a place, no matter how isolated a location. Just go to the coffee shop, sit in the public square. You will begin to see the diversity hidden in the most homogeneous of communities.

But what's more, even that isolated community is connected to all the rest of us by airwaves. And so, no matter where you live, you experience diversity through the media. I once talked to a government worker who served the Inuit communities in the farthest reaches of northern Canada. He described the scene to me: Igloos with antennas. "How can this be?" I asked. His answer: "Batteries!" How much more true this is for us. Get in your car, and turn on talk-radio. Curl up in bed, and tune in late-night TV. Settle into your airplane seat, and watch the video thoughtfully provided. You will notice the same thing: such amazing, astonishing diversity. It's enough to make you feel that nothing is for sure.

How can this diversity exist? What explains the tremendous differences that exist among us, differences of taste and, more important, differences of value?

The answer, I think, is simple: We feel differently because we've been different places. In the course of our lives, we have had very different experiences. These experiences have affected us. Indeed, they have become a permanent part of who we are. And these experiences have shaped our attitudes, our behavioral preferences, our typical reactions to events, our inclination to respond in particular ways. Because our experiences are different, we are different. And because we are different, our values are different as well.

Timothy E. O'Connell, Ph.D.

I'm not sure if this explanation takes care of everything. To be honest, I felt that these friends of mine also needed to be accused of "sin" for their reactions to that political speech. I was not prepared to excuse entirely their behavior, writing it off as the byproduct of their personal past. Deep down, I really felt (and I still do) that they ought to have repented of their nasty, condescending, judgmental attitudes.

But if past experiences don't explain everything, they do explain a lot. If they do not justify our personal faults, they do help explain why we are more susceptible to some faults than to others. And, on the other hand, if these experiences do not cancel out the beauty of our good qualities, they do make us a bit more humble. For the fact is that my "virtues" may say less about my "holiness" and more about the luck of the experiences I have had.

∽

I teach Christian ethics, and I am sometimes asked to explain exactly what that is. In some settings, where I can get away with it, I respond that Christian ethics is the systematic attempt of us Irish to live as if we were Italian! I rarely fail to get a laugh with this comment. There is just enough of a kernel of truth in it to spark a chuckle of recognition in my listeners. But recently I have modified my witty comment, responding to the observation of a good friend of mine, a man of Italian-American descent. "You don't understand, Tim," he said. "We Italians feel just as much guilt as you Irish. It's just about different stuff! You folks may be very uptight about sex, and we may appear casual about that. But we are incredibly uptight about family. My mother can make me feel terribly guilty, just asking me if I'm coming home for Sunday dinner!"

All of this is stereotype, of course. My point is not to characterize any particular group, it is simply to highlight three facts. First, we are all shaped by our past experiences. Secondly, our experiences are quite diverse. And thirdly, the results of these experiences are not always ideal. The old adage declares that the apple does not fall far from the tree. But if you have been near a cottonwood tree when it is shedding its fluff, you know that not every tree is altogether attractive. So we come out of our childhood shaped by our experiences in various ways, both good and bad.

Think of yourself. Surely you can trace the dotted lines from your attitudes and behaviors to those of the setting in which you were raised. And in many ways you may be thrilled by the connections that you see. Your sense of humor may have roots in the ways of your mother. Your delight in nature may have grown from summer camping trips into the wilds. Your compassion may be connected to the suffering you saw—or the suffering you endured—when you were young.

Or you may be disturbed by the connections that you see. Once, I was visiting my brother and his family. I was in the other room when my brother challenged one of his children. As I heard him, a shiver went down my spine. His voice was the stern, no-nonsense voice of my father. And while I have come to cherish the discipline I received from my father, the tone of voice my brother used raised in me a child's reaction to this large and demanding person. I mentioned it to my brother later, and he was troubled, too. "My heavens," he said. "I hadn't noticed that at all. But you're right. Those old ways are in us still."

As adults we have all sorts of feelings and reactions that are rooted in these past experiences of ours. We may be terribly sensitive to certain kinds of hurts, painfully shy in certain settings, embarrassingly inclined to shame around certain human behaviors. Or the opposite may be true. We may, in truth, be sadly oblivious to certain social niceties, destructively unconcerned about certain human problems, regrettably unmotivated to undertake certain valuable practices. And the reasons for this may have much to do with the past experiences that are ours.

The story is told that Marie Antoinette would leave the theater and step obliviously over the bodies of people starving in the street, all the time weeping over the death of the heroine in the opera she'd just seen. She just didn't notice.

And in so many areas the same may be said of us.

One of the major players in the Watergate scandal was Charles Colson. I don't have any information other than what I read in the papers, but it appears that he really did participate in the dirty tricks of the day. And a court of law thought so, too, for they sent him to jail. What was the result of this? As he has recounted in his writings since then, Chuck Colson got religion. Rather than staying locked in the perspectives of his past experiences, he allowed the experience of prison, unpleasant though it was, to touch him and shape him in new and different ways. Through this new experience, viewed through the lens of his deepening religious convictions, he became a new and different man.

Of course, the prison experience could have changed him in other ways, making him cynical and mean. As some have pointed out, U.S. prisons are often the world's most efficient training ground for criminals. So there was no guarantee that this particular experience would change him in this particular way. But it would make him different, of that there is no doubt.

Tend Your Own Garden

When I think of this phenomenon, I also think of those astronauts, who tell us that they have been forever changed by the sight of the planet Earth from the perspective of outer space. How could they ever again fall into the easy illusion that we humans are separable from each other? How could they focus only on their own needs, ignoring the needs of the person across the street, or across the ocean? The view from space makes clear how tiny those distances really are, how interconnected we all must be. And so this experience, this quiet experience of looking out a spaceship window, has changed people in ways that can never fade away.

I think of the hospital administrator who suddenly issued a set of changes in ordinary procedures, changes that established more flexible visiting hours, simplified the process of admission, offered alternative ways of preparing for surgery, and the like. What prompted this flurry of new ideas? She had undergone surgery herself! She had experienced what it was like to be a patient, and the experience had changed her inside. And because of that, she was motivated to change the way business was conducted.

I think of the students on the campus where I teach. Most of them are not rich by any means. Indeed, more than half of them belong to the first generation in their families to attend college. But in comparison with the whole human family, they are surely privileged. And so the campus ministry staff works hard to make sure the students know what it's really like out there in the "real world." And in one of their most powerful offerings, the staff provides a selection of "immersion trips," opportunities for the students to spend their spring break working with the poor and, more important, getting to know the poor as the persons that they are.

Timothy E. O'Connell, Ph.D.

Students go to Appalachia, to Belize, and to pockets of poverty right around the corner. They spend time with the people, often living with them and, paradoxically, enjoying their hospitality. They talk with the people, and watch them in the everyday conduct of their lives. The students also make a contribution, helping to build a church or clean a street or staff an overnight shelter. There is no illusion that their efforts will make much of a difference. Indeed, the immersion trips are not really about helping the poor. They are about providing experiences to the students.

And the experiences make a difference. The students do not generally change the direction of their lives, forsaking their career plans in favor of social service. In fact, it might not really be helpful if they did. But the students do move on with a different understanding, a different sensitivity, a different perspective. They take this experience into the career of their choice. And the hope of the organizers is that whatever the students eventually do, they will do it a bit differently because of the experience which the immersion trip provides.

Yes, if old experiences shape us, new experiences can help us change.

Something can be done: this is the final truth to be noticed here. God has blessed us not only with memories and events, God has also gifted us with reason. And while reason cannot guide our every moment (it would simply take too much work), reason can alert us to patterns that we would like to change. We can survey the terrain of our lives, and notice both the small issues that trouble us much too much and the big issues that we too easily overlook. Reason can highlight the contradictions between the pattern of our lives and the ideals we would like to espouse. Reason can give us a script for change.

And how is that change brought about? You surely have guessed the answer: We can open ourselves to new and different experiences. That is what's going on when the campus ministry staff takes the young people on their immersion trips, and we can do the same. We can structure situations where we will meet new people. We can watch instructive programs on television. We can sign up for enriching activities, whether they are academic courses in the nearby school or aerobic classes in the nearby gymnasium. We can, alas, read a new book!

Could it be, indeed, that part of what prompted you to pick up this book was the sense that something is not right in your life? Did the title start you wondering whether everything is as it should be and whether you are conducting your affairs as you really want to? I bet that is the case. And so, with a wisdom that human persons gloriously exhibit, you reached out for something new, for an experience that could make a difference.

It is interesting how I describe this. This book does not offer answers, rather it offers experiences. And if the book succeeds, these experiences will offer you new possibilities. They will complement and supplement and perhaps counterbalance the experiences of your past. And by so doing the new experiences that come to you in this book, and the new experiences you may be tempted to initiate as a result of reading this book, will provide you the opportunity for difference, for growth and change, for deepening and maturing.

The same is true of your children. Do you know the values you want them to embrace? Then give them experiences of those values. You want them to be compassionate? I know one family that carefully arranges opportunities for the children—and the adults—to work together in a soup kitchen, to gather clothing for the Thanksgiving drive. Do you want them to reverence knowledge? I know another family that makes a major event out of the moment when each child is eligible for her first library card, undertaking a formal trip to the library, choreographing the presentation of the card, inviting the newly mature child to show it to siblings and friends.

Provide experiences that express your values. And the experiences will deepen those values as well.

The opportunities that reside in new experiences are truly wonderful. But they are not without fear, either. Each fall I present a three-day workshop at a center where religious leaders go for renewal and continuing education. As part of my presentation, I discuss the point I'm making here: that new experiences offer us new possibilities. And then I invite them to recall the feelings with which they began the wonderful program in which they are engaged. I suggest that, as they arrived in this new place, they did not know how it would affect them, what new options it would offer and what new directions it would encourage. What they did know, beyond a shadow of a doubt, was that this program, this experience, would make them different. The person who would leave the program would be different than the person who entered it.

So as they began the program, even as they faced the uncertainties that are part of anything new, they had to say goodbye to the person they had been. They had to grieve its loss, even if the loss was a loss of attitudes and behaviors they didn't particularly like. For even bad habits can become old and comfortable friends. They had to let go of that old self. And they had to trust that the new experience, combined with the very positive strengths they had developed over the years, would promise a new self that would be a gift, and that would be worth the trouble it took.

One of my favorite movies is *Jeremiah Johnson,* an unusual sort of cowboy movie. At the end, Jeremiah, who has endured all sorts of sufferings and catastrophes, happens upon an old, wizened trapper. The trapper greets him, mentions that he has heard of Jeremiah's troubles, and offers him sympathies. "'Tweren't much trouble," replies Jeremiah. It's a massive understatement, of course. But it catches a deeper truth. Compared to the gift of new experiences, the trouble they involve isn't much trouble, at all.

The alternative to embracing new experiences, after all, letting go of the past and opening to the future, is death. And that is really trouble!

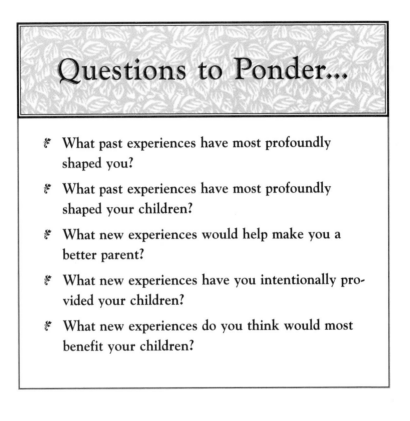

Questions to Ponder...

- ❦ What past experiences have most profoundly shaped you?

- ❦ What past experiences have most profoundly shaped your children?

- ❦ What new experiences would help make you a better parent?

- ❦ What new experiences have you intentionally provided your children?

- ❦ What new experiences do you think would most benefit your children?

3

Becoming Heroes

Heroes. We all have heroes. Let me tell you about several of mine.

My father, for example. He was a West Point man, ramrod straight, committed above all to honesty. "A cadet does not lie, steal, or cheat, or tolerate those who do, sir!" We memorized that declaration as children, and we never, ever, forgot it.

On one occasion I remember him coming home from work, sad because he had been forced to terminate an employee. I asked him how he went about it. He explained that a lot of people tended to beat around the bush, embarrassed to speak the bad news. But that struck him as mean, he told me. Instead, his way was to start with the bitter truth: "Your time here is over." About this decision there would be no discussion. But beyond this fact, he would say, all is discussible. "If you want to understand what you did wrong, we'll talk. If you want help in thinking about your future, we'll talk. If you want to see what can be learned from all this and what options may now be available, we'll talk. In fact, you can have all the time you want to explore these questions. For, even as you're leaving, you are important as a human person."

Timothy E. O'Connell, Ph.D.

That was his approach. It was, I thought, the way of a West Point man. He was a hero to me.

So was my grandmother. She was an opera lover. And I have a clear childhood memory of riding in the family car with her, the two of us trapped in the back seat. But I didn't mind. To fill the time, she was teaching me little snippets of various arias, tunes from the masterworks of the repertory. I go to the opera today, and it's a beautiful part of my life. For this interest I have my grandmother to thank.

When I think of heroes, I think of a man named Josef Fuchs. He is a German scholar, and I wrote my doctoral dissertation on his work. I liked his work, of course; otherwise, I wouldn't have chosen it as my topic. But what I most remember from my dissertation experience is learning about Josef Fuchs as a person. Early on I wrote him a letter, telling him that I was studying his scholarship. And he wrote back, wishing me luck. Near the end, I wrote again and asked if I could visit him to discuss some of my questions. He agreed immediately. I sent ahead a number of pages, summarizing my conclusions and observations, and then I went to Europe to meet him.

There he was, a tiny man, thin, with silver hair and the most delightful, warm smile. I don't remember much of the conversation we had that day. In fact, only a single memory remains clearly chiseled in my brain. "I have one demand, Tim," he said. "Don't make it sound like I'm dead. Point out that you're only studying the positions I've taken thus far. I reserve the right to change my mind."

Josef Fuchs was 61 when he said that. As I write these words he is still alive, now in his mid-eighties, still reserving the right to change his mind! And for that, he is a hero of mine.

Tend Your Own Garden

Heroes shape our lives. In the same way, we shape the lives of others when we become heroes to them. And there is a simple reason why this is true. All of us, no matter how old we are, have one important thing in common. What is that one thing? It is this: We have never been this age before! We may be young adults or mature persons bringing our lives to completion. It makes no difference; we have never been here before. We know more than we used to, of course. Life does help us grow. So, as we look back, we can notice our increasing skill and confidence, our wisdom and ability. But the job is not done. This is a new day, with new possibilities and new surprises. And we have never been here before.

So all of us begin every day of our lives with a small twinge of expectation, a sense that today life may present us with a challenge we don't know how to meet, may demand a skill we don't find within us. We begin every day with a sense of uncertainty, a sense even of insecurity. What do we do about this? We watch one another like hawks. We look around, seeking people who can show us how it's done. We look out ahead, seeking people who have been there before us. And, as we get older, we look back behind, seeking people who, because they are younger, may be more at home with the new challenges of the new and different day we now must face.

Yes, we watch each other like hawks. The patterns of our lives are developed through a process of observation and imitation. We all know this. Think of all the cute phrases people use. "Values are caught, not taught." "Your actions speak so loudly, I can't hear a word you're saying." "Children have no ears, but two sets of eyes." It's true: Growth in our lives occurs as a result of observation and imitation.

For children this process can be absolutely slavish. I'm embarrassed to recall—and I do recall it—coming home from the movie, *The*

Timothy E. O'Connell, Ph.D.

Three Musketeers. I was just a little boy. I slipped out the back door, into the yard. I found a broom handle. And raising my noble sword, I entered ferocious combat with my mortal enemies. Back and forth across the yard I ran, conquering first one evildoer and then another. In the end, I and my comrades, each of whom was clear to the eye of my mind, achieved victory complete. One for all and all for one! I was a Musketeer to the tips of my toes.

Or the process can, even for children, be more subtle and substantial. It may reveal more about my selfhood than I would like to acknowledge, when I describe the regular rhythm of my days as a school boy. My mother would drive me to school each morning. Then, having dropped me off, she would proceed to the parish church to attend daily Mass. She didn't talk about this practice of hers, she didn't explain it. She simply did it. But I was watching; I couldn't help but notice. And I have no doubt that observation and imitation have played a role in leading me to embrace religious values as central to human life. Heroes have that power.

Teenagers also engage in total imitation. The hero may be a sports celebrity. It may be a rock star. It may, sad to say, be a drug dealer. Suddenly, they begin to dress like the hero, to talk like the hero, to imitate the gestures and mannerisms, the attitudes and interests, the values and the visions of the hero.

As adults we become a bit more discriminating. We are not so likely to mold our whole life on the pattern of one individual. Instead, we are more likely to pick and choose, embracing the goals of one person, the techniques of another, the tastes of a third, and the causes of a fourth. But the process is the same.

As young adults, just entering the "real world," we look for guides. It may be a successful member of the firm or an experienced teammate on the work line. It may be another married person who balances home and job, personal life and parenting. It may be a supervisor or instructor, a neighbor or relative. No matter what the details, the basic truth is that these persons are guides for us. They serve us by just "doing their thing." And while they do it, we watch them like hawks. We learn from them the skills of adult living. We try out their ways of coping, their ways of succeeding. And through imitation (and later, variation), we develop in ourselves those same skills to become the adults we want to be.

These relationships are all temporary, of course. For we do, in the end, develop our own ways of succeeding. But where one hero is left behind, another is quickly found, as we confront the successive challenges of human living. How do you handle having a teenager? What do you do as your youthful energy turns into mid-life fatigue? How can you let go of those you love, of the parents who raised you, the siblings who have always been at your side? What do you do as your own mortality becomes more obvious, your eventual death more inescapable? To answer these questions, we watch one another like hawks. We watch, and our observation leads to imitation. And this, in turn, leads to the unique journey that is each of our lives.

We build our lives through a process of observation and imitation. And so do the children we love. So passing along the value priorities that we cherish is not, in the first instance, a matter of instruction. In fact, the verbal communication of values is among the least important components of the process. It does have a role, as we'll see later, but it's not really central. We don't shape our lives on the ideas we are taught. Rather we shape our lives in imitation of the heroes we have found.

Timothy E. O'Connell, Ph. D.

It's not what you say; it's who you are. Here's the important lesson for us to learn. If I want to influence my children, if I want to pass along to them the value priorities which I believe to be right, then the most important thing is to be sure those priorities are really mine. Do I live those priorities? Are they evident in my everyday life? Or are they just the cheap talk with which I muddy the field of my life?

I tell the children not to use vulgar phrases, and I avoid using those phrases in front of the children. I do use them, of course, but only when I'm off with the grown-ups. I tell the children not to pick on their playmates, and I don't pick on my spouse. But in my career, my approach is to compete with everyone, collaborate with no one, and in a conflict to give no quarter. What do I teach the children? Good taste? Concern for others? No. I teach them hypocrisy. And have no doubt. Sooner or later they will see the real me, and sooner or later they will get the real lesson.

I say that I stand for honesty, for fair play, for compassion. I say that life demands hard work, that beauty should be admired, that relationships are more important than possessions. The children will not listen to my words; they will observe my everyday behavior. They will see how I spend my time and my money. They will notice what gets preference in the inevitable choices that life demands. They will monitor how I react as I watch a sporting event or participate in a so-called recreational activity. All this will tell them the truth. This will show them my true values. And this—the truths they observe in my behavior—is what will feed the values already growing within them.

It's who you are. So tend your own garden, making sure it's filled with beauty and not with weeds.

Tend Your Own Garden

Even when you tend your own garden, sad to say, there's no guarantee that your example will win the day. We live in a big world, and many people are competing for the role of hero in the lives of your children. Think of all the people in your everyday life. You encounter a pastor, a rabbi, an imam, or monk. You encounter a concerned neighbor organizing the block party, shoveling the walk, and cutting the lawn of the elderly lady down the street. You have friends who volunteer at the soup kitchen, serve as den mothers or soccer coaches.

But you also experience, as I did, the man who finds your car keys, and then charges you for giving them back. You meet the construction contractor who cuts corners, and brags about how rich he's becoming. You deal with the grumpy check-out lady, the disinterested salesperson, the aggressive and endangering automobile driver.

And there is the bigger world, the one we encounter second-hand. Political leaders take initiatives that improve our lives and protect our peace. Then they waste our money and abuse our trust. Athletes demonstrate strength and courage, perseverance and grace. Then they exhibit self indulgence and immaturity, viciousness and unconcern. You need only turn on some of the daily talk shows to discover that the spirit of the ancient coliseums, where slaughter was organized for the entertainment of the masses, is alive and well in our time.

Who will be your children's heroes? The range of possibilities is great. And each of us is, in the end, free to look where we will and embrace what we like. So all our efforts to present positive heroes cannot guarantee success. We can only do our best, tending our gardens, working truly to be the sorts of people we claim to value.

41

We can only be heroes to ourselves, in the hopes that the observation of the children we love will see and embrace who we are.

~

My suggestion is that you conduct a "hero audit." It's embarrassing, to say the least. But it is important. Forget about the people you want to influence. Forget about the children you want to mold. Forget about your clients and customers, your friends and family. Look only at yourself. And ask yourself that frightening question: "Am I a hero to myself?"

Look across the whole range of your life. Look at your work life. Recall your behavior in the office or plant. Look at the times when you interact with others. But even more important, look at the moments when you are alone. Are you a hero to yourself?

Look at your family life. Review your time with those you love. Is it quantity time? Is it quality time? Are you a hero to yourself?

Look at how you "spend" your life, its time and its money. Are you sharing or hoarding, giving back or merely collecting? Are you a hero to yourself?

And look at your life, your central, utterly personal life as a citizen of the universe. How do you fit in? Are you raging against the dark or reaching for the stars? Have you stayed faithful to your deepest dreams, or have you settled for quiet desperation? Is there adoration in your life, and awe, or merely cynical and apathetic indifference? Are you a hero to yourself?

Yes, conduct a hero audit. And when you have, make a plan that is based on what you learn.

Tend Your Own Garden

Do this if you care about yourself. Do this if you don't. Do this if you care only about the children. For in the end, your best chance of influencing the children is by presenting them with heroes. And the best hero you can present them is you. You are nearby. You are the one they watch the most. You care. You are the one they love the most. You, of all people, should be a hero to the children you love.

You will never be their only hero, of course. And in the end, despite your best efforts, you may not be the hero they embrace. But if you care, you surely must try. And if you try, you can be confident that it will be noticed. And some time, in some way, it will surely make a difference.

So whatever your age, whatever your circumstance, always be a hero to yourself.

And then let that beauty show!

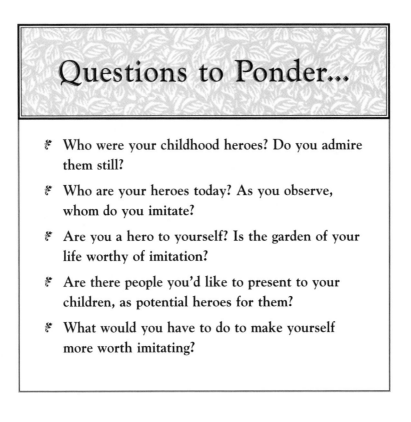

Questions to Ponder...

❦ Who were your childhood heroes? Do you admire them still?

❦ Who are your heroes today? As you observe, whom do you imitate?

❦ Are you a hero to yourself? Is the garden of your life worthy of imitation?

❦ Are there people you'd like to present to your children, as potential heroes for them?

❦ What would you have to do to make yourself more worth imitating?

4

Gotta Have A Gang

"Gang."

Isn't it interesting, the different connotations that word has? It has an ugly meaning, pointing at groups of youth out of control, causing mayhem and suffering to all around. We talk about the problem of gang violence in our cities. Parents struggle mightily to keep their children out of gangs. We are shocked to hear about the methods of recruitment, the bizarre and horrible rites of initiation, the utter control exercised by leaders and the savage acts undertaken obediently by foot soldiers. Those terrible gangs!

But then there's the older meaning of the word. "Wedding bells are breaking up that old gang of mine," said the song, and the image was of a warm, valued group of friends. "The whole gang is going out for pizza!" "Mom, if we move, I'll leave my gang behind and I won't have anyone!" How important to children to have a gang, to feel linked to loyal and interested friends.

What's true of children is true of us all, of every human person: You gotta have a gang.

Over the years, as I have been studying how people's values are passed on to others, one discovery has stood out. It is this: The native soil of values isn't the individual person, it's the group. It's not that values reside within the person and are transmitted from the person to the group. In a way, the process of value transmission can look like that. But as we look more closely, that's not really how it works. Rather, it's the other way around. Values reside in groups. And it is the group that conveys the values to the individual members.

How a particular group comes to embrace particular values isn't clear. Sometimes the leadership of a dynamic individual (shaped, in turn, by some previous group) may play a role. Other times strong traditions may leave little doubt about what those values will be. But however they come to birth, the values take root in the garden of the group, and the group, as a group, becomes the soil in which they grow. Then when new individuals come into the group, they soon discover the group's values. And if they stick around long enough, the group's values finally become their values, too.

When the newly arrived individual finds a harmony between the values received from past groups and the commitments of this new group, she or he feels immediately at home. So the individual likely chooses to stay in this new group, to become a member and participate in its life. Simultaneously, the group welcomes the new member precisely because this new person is seen to harmonize with the values of the group. The result, then, for this new individual is that these personal values, the values of the group, are reinforced and deepened within him or her.

But another scenario is possible. This newly arrived individual may find himself or herself at odds with the values of the group. The values of this new group are not the values of the groups of the past. Perhaps the new group drinks, while the old group didn't. Or the new group values participating in church activities, while the old group had no religious tone at all. No matter the exact details of the differences, the basic reality is the same: This group's values are not the values of my past. In such a case, only two outcomes are possible. Either the individual will leave the group, protecting the past values by finding some other group more sympathetic to them. Or the individual will abandon those past commitments and embrace the values of these new friends. Nothing else is possible.

I know a family who generously agreed to house a young man from another city who wished to attend the local college. He seemed quite committed to this project, and looked forward to it for over a year. But in the end, after less than two semesters, he abandoned the idea, moved out, got a job, and eventually returned home. Why did this happen? My friends reflected long and hard over the experience. Had they failed to offer enough support? Had they misunderstood the youth's desires? No, the answer, they decided, lay elsewhere.

The young man said that he wanted to attend college, and he was sincere in saying so. But in fact, almost no one in his family had ever gone to college. He had never been close to anyone who had survived the gauntlet of college study and learning. He had no heroes to observe up close. What is more, his core groups, both the family and his long-time friends, did not have a tradition of going to college. So, while they might speak words of support, their behavior did not show that this was a value of the group.

Then, as the young man began his college career, he developed a pattern of running to school, leaving immediately after class for his part-time job, and then coming home to eat and sleep. He did eventually make a few friends. But lo and behold, one quit school before he did, and the other settled for an occasional course, scheduled around her full-time job.

In a word, this young man never found a group of college-believers among whom to set down roots. He never found a group which truly espoused this value. And in the absence of such a group, it was probably just a matter of time before he abandoned his plans for education.

Yes, the native home of values is groups, and groups give the values to their members.

❡

If values live in groups and groups pass their values to their members, this is particularly true in the case of families. For families, after all, are nature's first and foremost group.

The case of families is complicated, however. Since children grow into adulthood in part by separating themselves from their families, by defining themselves over and against their families, the patterns of value-transmission are not always obvious in this setting. Harried parents, besieged by the "No's" of the terrible twos or by the obsessive privacy of adolescence, may despair that any values are being passed along. But the family is, in the end, a group like any other. And for better or worse, the values of the group are finding their way into the hearts of all the members.

Some time ago I was enjoying dinner at a local restaurant. At a table across the room was a family, out for a celebration of someone's birthday. But what an odd family! Most of the members were conservatively dressed, the men with close-cropped hair and the women with outfits in subdued colors. And then there was the teen-age daughter. Her hair was purple, spiked up in the center and shaved close around the ears. Several pierced earrings adorned her left ear. She wore loose-fitting clothes that reminded me of "Joseph's coat of

48

many colors." Indeed, the clothes seemed more like rags, sewn together and shaped to cover her body.

I had such mixed emotions. On the one hand, I was repulsed by the daughter's appearance. I wondered how the family could dare to be in public with this young woman. But then, upon further thought, I felt great admiration for the family. They were carrying on nonetheless. And, truth to tell, they all seemed to be having a fine time, even the daughter who was joining in the conversation, laughing at the jokes and responding to the comments. I thought to myself, "This is going to turn out OK. These parents have defined the group of their family by what is really, finally important: sharing and caring. The daughter will get through this rebellious moment. And when she does, she will have memories of a group that expressed values that can deeply, wonderfully guide her life."

Yes, although they may look a bit different, families are groups like any other. When the rebellious phase is over and the dust settles, it is amazing how often we see in the children precisely the values that were important to the parents. We see lifestyles that are similar, priorities that are unchanged, preferences that survive for generations on end. So parents shouldn't panic. Stay true to your values. In the long run if not immediately, chances are those values will become your children's values, too.

Still, there is another factor here. After all, we don't belong to just one group. Especially in the case of families, it is inevitable that children will grow up, move out, encounter and then join other groups. And as they do so, the children will change. They will embrace the values of these other groups. In so doing, they may let go of the values of the family. As the family fades into the background and life is built around other groups, friends, work colleagues, spouses and life partners, the child will become different.

Nothing proves the point better than the awful experience of family reunions. Have you felt the tension of these events? The children, now adults, come home for the holiday. And in so doing the self-of-today, the self that is shaped by the groups to which it belongs here and now, encounters the self-of-the-past, the self that once existed, that was shaped almost entirely by the values of the family where it grew up. Ah, the tension of the thing! Shall I go to church to pacify Mom? What do I say when Dad spouts his usual political commentary, espousing positions I reject entirely? And what about my brother, who has finally made peace with the fact that he is gay? What shall I do about that? All the while, Mom and Dad, who feel that they haven't changed and can't understand why everyone else has, try to decide whether to keep silent—or scream at the top of their lungs!

The situation is amusing in some ways. In fact, this kind of thing is a regular topic for motion pictures precisely because it is both familiar and funny. But it's sad, too. For this diverging of values represents a death of the family as it once was. It is no longer really a group for its members. It is no longer the place where its members truly live, where they receive their values and have them reinforced. Love may still exist. There may be gratitude for gifts received and commitment to return care and concern. But in a very real sense, as a group, as a family unit, this family is dead. It has done its work, and its time is over.

This truth about groups, that they are the true home of values, is seen in business settings, too. Sometimes we think we can do our job with no attention to the values of the organization where we work. And I suppose it's true that in a crisis one can hunker down, ignore those nearby, and focus only on the task at hand. If the only alternative is to starve, one can do almost anything.

But in the long run such a thing just doesn't work. I have been told that among medical doctors, more than half of them abandon their first work location within five years of starting it. That is, fresh from training, they tend to select a group practice or a hospital location or a health provider firm for financial reasons, or perhaps because of its location. But then, after a few years, conflicts between the individual doctor's values and those of the organization become unbearable. The doctor realizes slowly that either a move must occur, or the doctor's values will change. So these young physicians go searching for an alternative location, and this time the criteria are not only money and location. Now one of the criteria is harmony of overall vision. They look for other doctors, or for health care providers, whose philosophy of medicine meshes with the one they received from their previous groups. And when they find this, they set out to join and make this their place of work.

The same thing happens to lots of people, in many different lines of work. I have a friend who is an architect. For a while he worked for one particular firm, and he was successful in this setting. But the leader of this organization was a man for whom profit was the only value, and he regularly demanded all sorts of unethical compromises. They would double-bill clients, cut deals with suppliers, and in a hundred ways strive to make money no matter what. Eventually my friend came to the conclusion that he had to get out. And at a moment of crisis, he quit cold, with no other job to go to, no alternative in place.

Of course, he had the strength to do this in large part because of his other groups. His family and friends supported him in his values, confirmed to him that he was right, assured him that he was doing the right thing, and promised to stand by him in this difficult moment. And so, with that strength received from others, he was able to shake the dust from his feet and move on.

What happened? I'm delighted to report that my friend's reputation as a person of principle spread through the professional community, and before long he was offered an outstanding job. I know that things do not always work out so well. And it is important to remember that, in his moment of courageous action, he himself did not know it would work out so well. Still, it is encouraging to know that even in the world of business, honesty and fairness are appreciated and that people of virtue can still be professionally successful.

So the truth is confirmed: Values are found in groups, and groups pass them along to their members. As this is true of the family and of the business group, it is also true of friendship groups. I enjoy watching the young women and men make friends as they arrive at the university where I teach. The process is very quick; often within hours of arriving, the new students have affiliated with others and convened themselves into little groups of friends. And the result is that, at least for the moment, they have a place to "hang out."

But very often these friendships don't last. As time goes on, differences of values become more evident. Often the difference has to do with social behavior, especially drinking or sexual behavior. It may have to do with money, how much one has and how much one spends. And related to this, it may have to do with where one goes, the kinds of vacation one takes and so on. Or it may be different attitudes toward study, whether education is to be taken seriously or not. It may involve what we call "academic integrity," whether or not to try to cheat on an exam or to plagiarize a term paper.

In any case, a conflict becomes clear, between the individual and the group, or perhaps more accurately between this new group and the old groups to which the individual has belonged and to which she or he remains committed. And the universal question inevitably arises: Shall I stay in this group and change my values to match theirs? Or shall I seek a group whose values more closely match those I've received and embraced in the past? And as always, only two alternatives are possible. The individual moves on, or the individual changes.

So, for example, at the end of freshman year there is a massive migration, as students break up the original, assigned dorm-room groups and reconvene in groups of genuinely shared values.

∽

These ideas are not just a description of what has already happened. They are also a challenge for action in the future. And I mean this in several different ways.

First, there is the challenge to each of us as individuals. The truth is that we will become an expression of the groups to which we belong. So we need to look carefully at those groups. Is this who I really want to be? Is this the direction I want my life to take?

Second, there is the challenge to us as people who want to pass on our values. Our most successful strategy will not involve a lot of shouting about how one ought to live. It will not be direct intervention into the life of the one we hope to influence. Rather, our most powerful weapons are the groups we create. Value transmitters are group conveners. Bring together a group of like-minded individuals. Allow them to reinforce one another's values as the values set down roots in the soil of the group. And trust the reality of the group to teach the individuals what it means to be a particular sort of person.

Third, there is the challenge to us as people who are sometimes responsible for groups. If you are a parent, you are responsible for a group. If you are a teacher, you are responsible for a group. If you are a religious leader or an employer or an elected official, you are responsible for a group. And if you are any of these, then the challenge is clear: tend to the health of your group. A group's values can change. If an unusually strong individual enters the group, they can prompt a modification in the group's values. And even in a group whose members remain the same, the ebb and flow of life experiences can lead to a slow erosion of the group's values.

The simple truth is that the group that stands for nothing . . . stands for nothing! So groups need to defend their values. On occasion they need to be forceful in saying what their values are. "This is what we stand for, this is what we believe in. If you want to be one of us, these values must be your values, too. Otherwise, move on, find some other group in which to dwell."

This is not fun, but it is important. If you want to be a leader, convene a group, cultivate a group. And defend that group when necessary.

For the home of values is groups. And protecting the home is the most important thing.

∽∾∽∾∽∾

Questions to Ponder...

* Do you see your family of origin in yourself? Do you like what you see?

* Where your family of origin is less than ideal, have you found other groups to support the values you prefer?

* Is your family, as it now exists, the proper soil for the values you hope to pass on to your children?

* Are your children in the kind of groups that will support the values you espouse?

* If you had the chance to create a group that would stand for your values, what would it look like? Whom would it include?

5

Practice Makes Permanent

When I was a child, my grade school education involved lots of memorizing. We learned to read and write through phonics. We learned our multiplication tables by singing "two-times-two-is-four," and so on. We diagrammed sentences, parsed verbs, recited historical dates. We listed state capitals, kings of England, and agricultural specialties. And we did all of this over and over again.

Then came the shift away from rote learning. Experts realized that all this memorizing had a down-side: that students sometimes didn't understand what they were learning. When all their focus was on just remembering the various facts, children didn't develop the skills of insight and assessment. They didn't grasp the significance of the information they were absorbing. As a result, they really couldn't use the information. And since it wasn't useful, it quickly became irrelevant, and then it was lost altogether. After all, what can be memorized can just as easily be forgotten.

There is much to be said in support of this criticism, much to be said for an approach to learning that emphasizes genuine understanding. And probably, on balance, the changes in teaching methods that resulted from this reassessment have improved the education of our children. But something was lost, too, I think.

Timothy E. O'Connell, Ph.D.

Curiously enough, while the educational practice of simple repetition departed the classroom, it never left the school entirely. It survived in the gym! A truth that the teachers sometimes forgot was always remembered by the coaches: Some skills are developed only by doing, and doing over and over again. It is true that there is a thing called "teaching." Even in sports, there are moments for sitting the team down in front of the blackboard and explaining to them the theory of the game, the underlying pattern of the play. But there is also something else, called "training," and it is central to successful athletic experiences. In the end there is no substitute for practice.

For seven years, when I was in grammar school, I took piano lessons. I am willing to confess this fact to you, good reader, precisely because I'll probably never meet you in the vicinity of a keyboard. I'll never have to justify this investment of my parents' money and my time. I'm not sure I could. Oh, I loved music, and I love it still. And I did develop some skills at casual playing that I still use. But I don't think my level of playing sounds like the possession of a person with seven years of lessons. And why is that? Because I didn't practice.

If I use these pages to speak the lesson of practice's important role, my conviction is partly born of my own mistakes. I didn't practice. I didn't persevere in the rigorous repetitions that alone can produce real skill at playing the piano. I didn't work on my scales, I didn't study my etudes. I didn't struggle with the daily exercises that would have trained my fingers and my eyes in the reading and performing of piano music.

I didn't practice. And for that very reason, I know better than most and as well as any that nothing but practice will work. Nothing but practice will develop those skills and habits that enrich our daily lives. For if practice does not make perfect, at least it does make easier—and better.

And eventually, practice makes permanent.

Several years ago, I attempted to teach my nephew how to drive a car. It was a challenging project, taxing my patience and his humility. I drove the car to a nearby city park. It was off-season, and the place was deserted. I pulled into a large parking lot, assured myself that we had the place to ourselves, and let him take over. Back and forth we drove, going slowly down one aisle, turning hesitantly at the end, and coming back down the next row. For more than an hour we did this. And we did it for several successive evenings. How slowly he learned!

I was fascinated by the process of it all. There really weren't any words I could speak that would quickly teach him how to drive. Oh, I could give advice. But even here, I found that too many words could confuse him as well as too few. In the end, he had to feel it in his muscles and then train his muscles to do it automatically. And there really was no way to short circuit the laborious process through which the learning would take place.

The same process can be seen in more subtle areas of life. A friend of mine, a psychologist, once told me about a challenge he faced in his counseling. He did quite a bit of work with adolescents. And he found that they often complained about their loneliness, the lack of friends, the absence of anyone with whom to share their lives. For a while, in his counseling, my friend would pursue the traditional avenues of exploration and understanding. He would help them see the reasons for their insecurity, its roots in their past experiences and its tendency to subvert their present desires. And sometimes this conversation was sufficient to lead the young person to change.

Timothy E. O'Connell, Ph.D.

But sometimes, he told me, this conversation led nowhere at all. It seemed to just spin around on its own axis, evolving from healthy introspection to useless navel-gazing. And in those cases, he found it far more helpful to stop this exploration, to shift instead to a quite different therapeutic approach.

"Listen," he would say. "Let's stop worrying about why you feel the way you do. Let's just try to do something to change it. Oh, I realize you can't change all at once. But you can change a little. So when we next meet, I don't want to hear your latest thoughts on the experience of your loneliness. Instead, I want to hear about one step you've taken to improve your situation. I want you to take the initiative by saying hello to one person. I want you to invite one person to go to a movie with you. I want you to pay one person an unsolicited compliment. One way or another, I want you to do one thing to move your experience in a new and better direction. And then when we get together, I want us to talk about what that was like."

You can imagine how helpful this approach would be in such cases. The old aphorism declares that the longest journey begins with a single step. And these small, tentative steps in the direction of making friends became the building blocks for a whole new approach to living. It was a matter of practice.

These kinds of rote and mechanical enactment work also with the values that should shape our lives. Think of some of the values you often affirm for yourself and for those you love: honesty, compassion, fairness, commitment, and the like. Now look at those words. Do they look familiar? They should. They are ancient words, that belong to an ancient category. They are virtues.

But what are virtues? Scholars say that virtues are "moral habits." That is, they are habits of life, habits characteristic of good persons. And what are habits? They are inclinations and abilities to do something. That is, habits are integrated skills. They may involve the skills of playing basketball. Michael Jordan has a masterful habit of playing basketball. They may involve the skills of flying a plane, using a computer, writing a poem. In every case habits involve the joining of inclination to ability, with the result that the person has a skill woven deeply into the character of the self. And virtues are moral habits.

Another way to put this is to say that virtues are human strengths. The word "virtue" comes from the Latin word *virtus*, which means "strength." So virtues are strengths, capacities to act in particular ways in a variety of circumstances. But how do we become strong? Through exercise, of course. Just as we use the muscles of the human body so that they will become stronger, more able to do the tasks we ask of them, so the same thing is true here. We use the muscles of our human spirit; and in the using they become stronger, more able to lift heavy burdens and move stubborn loads. One instance of telling the truth in a difficult situation makes it easier to tell the truth next time. One moment of gentleness in the face of unfair attack makes it easier to live gently all the time.

I remember with embarrassment a time when I was playing with several of my friends. I think we boys were all about eight or nine years old. Down the street a new house was being built. Excavating the foundation had produced a high mound of soil, a mountain, it seemed to us. And we simply had to climb it. Once at the top we surveyed our kingdom and celebrated our power. That's when several girls walked by. How dare they traverse our territory without permission! So we started to pelt them with clods of mud from our mountain.

Needless to say, within hours the entire story had found its way through the neighborhood telegraph to my mother. Her reaction was instantaneous. "Did you boys throw dirt at the girls?" After some hesitation I admitted we had. "Well, that's not right. I will not have you doing that. Right now, you are marching down the street to apologize to the girls. And you are going to tell them that you won't do it any more."

Was this intervention really influential in my life? Well, I still remember it! And I think I'm a little less inclined to throw dirt—in any sense of that term—as a result of this childhood experience.

Wise parents provide this sort of training all the time, getting their children to act with virtue and thereby developing the abilities to do so on a regular basis. "I know you don't feel like doing your homework right now. You'd rather go out and play. But I want you to stick to the work for another half hour. Then you can join your friends down the street." "I know you don't like the sweater your grandmother sent you for Christmas. But she gave it to you out of love. So you will write her a thank-you note nonetheless." "I know you've received a last-minute invitation to go on this exciting weekend trip. But when you agreed to join the soccer team you made a commitment to your teammates. You don't have to play soccer next year if you don't want to. But for this year you made a commitment, and you must fulfill it. So you cannot skip the game to go on the trip."

These small experiences are not profoundly life-changing. They are just tiny instances of practice. But as any coach will tell you, it takes hours and hours of practice, each repetition making its tiny contribution, before the skill is firmly woven into the fabric of the athlete's behavior. And the same is true here. Those of us who wish to pass along the values that we cherish must urge our charges to do the good thing, to do it over and over, to do it until it becomes automatic, to do it until it becomes part of the self. Then, and only then, will the person be truly, integrally, virtuous.

We must see ourselves not only as teachers. We are coaches as well. I love that word, "coach," to describe our role in cultivating virtues in those we love. To be a coach, as we've seen, is to challenge people to behave in a particular way and then to help them practice until they develop the skill and the strength to do it. Describing ourselves as coaches highlights this pattern of challenge and practice. Calling ourselves coaches spotlights one other idea, too: it reminds us that those we seek to influence still remain in charge of their own lives. It is their life, not mine. Just as the basketball players are on the court, with the coach contributing from the sidelines, so our children are on the court of their lives and we contribute only from the side.

We need to encourage them to go onto that court. As a teacher, I often stand in the front of the room. I do the talking, making notes on the blackboard. The students sit expectantly and focus on me as I "do my thing." And for some kinds of learning, that is fine. But not for the learning of virtues. For this to happen, the learners must come to the front, must begin to act, must take the lead and do the work. And I must shift from the role of teacher to that of coach. I must move to the sidelines, making suggestions, organizing routines of practice, offering encouragement. But not taking over, most certainly not stealing the ball and reclaiming the playing of the game. No, it's their game and it's their life. And they must do the work.

Timothy E. O'Connell, Ph.D.

One summer, as I was visiting another college to teach a summer-school course, I met an expert in educational theory. I asked for her help so I could improve my teaching. She agreed, and several days later announced that she had some comments to share. I wondered how she had come to acquire these ideas, and she told me she'd listened to my class from outside the door. On the basis of this observation she had advice to offer. "Your problem," she told me, "is that you fundamentally misunderstand your job! You think you're paid to teach. Actually, you're paid to help people learn!"

Her insight has profoundly, and permanently, changed my approach to teaching. It is not my job to fill the time with words, to drown my students in information that may be important to me but that is unconnected to them. It is my job to do whatever I can—including being silent, on occasion—to help them in the process of their learning. I must use my skill, but they are ultimately in charge.

It reminds me of the common childhood complaint: "Mother, please! I'd rather do it myself!" Those of us who are parents know how hard it is to honor that desire. We can do it better. Of course we can. In most regards, we have been here longer, have done it more, have practiced it and honed it more fully. So of course we can do most things better than they can. But the goal, in most really important things in life, is not to get it done. The goal is to learn to do it. And for that, they must do it themselves!

So we must accept our role as coaches. We must imagine ourselves on the sidelines, cheering and advising but never taking over. And as coaches, we must guide our charges through the steps of practice that will build up in them the strengths of spirit that should characterize their lives.

Tend Your Own Garden

Scholars tell us that in one important dimension, the development of skills for human living differs from the acquisition of sports abilities. As humans we have bodies that need to develop these strengths through practice. But we also have minds. And so, without contradicting all this, we also need to understand. Indeed, there is such an interweaving of the parts of the human person, that even the rote practice that helps our strengths to grow works better if we also understand.

One scholar has said that, in the end, the best strategy for helping people grow as persons is an ongoing combination of two things: expectation and explanation. On the one hand, we need to demand of those we are raising that they behave in certain ways. "I know you don't like it, but still you must do it. You must finish your homework, write a letter to your Aunt Louise, go to church with the family, replace the window that you broke, return the candy that you stole, postpone playing till the family dinner is through." But on the other hand, we need to take the extra time to explain why we value these particular ways of acting, why we believe they will be helpful to the child, why we hope they will eventually become integrated virtues they will embrace on their own. "You must do this because . . . ."

So, in the end, we are both teachers and coaches, agents of explanation and of expectation, providers of information and designers of practice. For in the case of this strange animal called the human person, both sides of this coin are needed if we are to become truly strong, if we are to become the women and men of virtue that we dream we could be.

Timothy E. O'Connell, Ph. D.

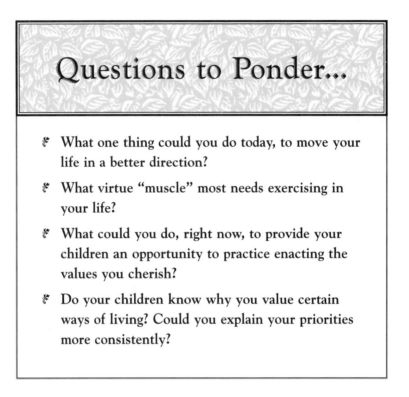

Questions to Ponder...

- ☙ What one thing could you do today, to move your life in a better direction?

- ☙ What virtue "muscle" most needs exercising in your life?

- ☙ What could you do, right now, to provide your children an opportunity to practice enacting the values you cherish?

- ☙ Do your children know why you value certain ways of living? Could you explain your priorities more consistently?

6

Tell Me A Story

"Mommy, tell me a story."

Everybody loves a story. Certainly the children do. It is amazing how important the stories are to children. They curl up in bed, snuggling against the pillow. Mom or Dad begins the story, "Once upon a time." The magical process begins again.

It may be a "true story." There once was a little boy, barely five years old, whose pants caught on fire when he jumped over a bonfire. The blaze was extinguished by his older brother, who chased him, tackled him, and rolled him in the grass till the flames were snuffed out. Years later, nothing could better calm this brother's children, assuring them that they were safe in the protection of a powerful and loving man, than the recounting of this powerful story. "Daddy, tell us about the time you saved Uncle Tim's life."

Sometimes it's a "made-up story." Recall how Little Red Riding Hood struggled with danger on the way to Grandmother's house, how Jack climbed the beanstalk and conquered the Giant, how Cinderella got to attend the ball and finally met the Prince of her dreams. Several years ago, a Broadway musical, *Into the Woods*, revisited these wonderful stories and illumined the way they speak a truth for the child inside all of us. Every child is, in a thousand different ways, required to go into the woods of their lives, to wrestle with the demons found there, and to trust that they will, in the end, return safely, getting home before dark. How true, how true!

So children love stories, factual or otherwise. And the stories they seek don't have to be new stories, either. Quite the contrary, old stories often seem preferable; tonight's story can be the same one that was told last night. For it isn't the conveying of information that is central to a good story. No, it is the telling and hearing of the story, the process itself that is the heart of the power of stories in our lives.

And what is that power? It is the power to transmit the values that define and shape the lives we seek to lead.

Stories are not just for children, either. Recently I attended a dinner party organized by a relative of mine when I visited her town. Among the guests were two persons who were meeting for the first time. One was a Catholic nun, a woman of great competence who had lived in this town for thirty-five years, providing a wide range of important services. The other was a retired realtor, a man who had been active in this community for over forty years and who, in the course of his work, had interacted with almost all the local leaders.

How intriguing the conversation became. She would say, "I saw Mrs. So-And-So in the hospital the other day." He would reply, "Oh yes, I know her. I sold her husband the house over on Blankity-Blank Street. Did you know that he donated the land on which the town hall now stands?" Or he would say, "I was invited by Miss Elegant to appraise her house, back when Senator Ratfink divorced her. She certainly is an amazing woman." To which Sister would reply, "She certainly is. I have lunch with her each month, and she's doing quite well after her knee surgery."

The hostess and I listened intently, spellbound by the weaving of these stories of the town, acquiring all sorts of information about the local scene. But more intriguing was what we heard between the lines, picking up the flavor of the community, the energy and attitudes that have shaped this town over the decades. I left the party understanding this town in ways I never had before, despite many previous visits.

Ah, the power of stories! Since the dawn of history, people like us have been gathering to share the stories that define who we really are. In the ancient world we gathered around a campfire, fending off the cold and the dark with the warmth and light that came as surely from the stories as from the embers. Grandparents told how it used to be, in the days before we were born. Wise leaders recounted the stories of how it had been in the beginning, when the primeval forces of good and evil had first competed. Hunters told stories of the struggle to fell the beast, to bring home the meat that would feed the family through the winter. And in a precursor of today's stories of fishing and golfing, the hunters could be forgiven if the beast grew a bit larger in the telling, if the risk of the hunt became a bit more fearsome.

Today, our stories may be told around the dinner table instead of the campfire. Or we may tell our stories with the help of technology, aided by the oral historian who visits the retirement home, tape recorder in hand, to quiz the old-timers about their memories and their myths. Or we may luxuriate in the technicolor renditions of our stories, as packaged and presented by Hollywood. I am struck by the fact that, in the fall of 1997, with all the completely made-up stories that were presented for our entertainment, among the most noteworthy movies were *Titanic* and *Amistad*, both joining historical fact to deeper human truth and thereby enacting the ancient human tradition wherein we tell our stories to one another.

Why are stories so important? Why do they touch us so deeply? Scholars have wrestled with this question. And the answers they have found are beautiful, exciting answers, answers that can be a gift to us in our lives. What are those answers?

If I tell you, quite baldly, that Patrick loves Margaret, I offer you nothing more than a bare fact. And with this fact you can do nothing; you can only file it away next to the other unimportant, unconnected facts that clog the synapses of your brain. But if I tell you about the night the house caught fire, that is something else altogether. . . .

There is Patrick, running down the street, weaving between the tall oaks that line the block of city homes, jumping over the hoses that snake from the red, growling pumpers to the front lawn of the house where Margaret lives. He's only seventeen, of course. But that doesn't mean he doesn't love. And now he is prepared to prove it.

Patrick dashes across the lawn, takes the front steps two at a time. Ignoring the shouts of the firemen he pushes through the front door and heads for the basement stairs. There is a moment of silence, a breathless instant of waiting as the bystanders try to make sense of the scene. What is going on? Will Patrick's audacious act bring him to harm? Why is he doing this?

Then Patrick reappears, running back down the steps almost before we realize he is there. He is safe! And there, in his arms, is Margaret, little, terrified beagle puppy that she is. And she seems to be hugging

Patrick, rather than the other way around. She loves him, and for a very simple reason. He has loved her first, and has proved his love through risky, actually foolish but still wonderful, acts of care and compassion. He—he alone—knew that Margaret was leashed in the basement, a part of the process of housebreaking her. And knowing that, he acted. And thus his love shone forth. . . .

Yes, if I tell you quite baldly that Patrick loves Margaret, I offer you nothing more than a bare fact, sterile and useless. But if I tell you a story, I do much more. I appeal to your imagination. I set you picturing the events I describe. And to the extent that I help you see those events, taste and feel them in your mind, I give you the very experience that I describe. Now, you do not simply know for a fact that Patrick loves Margaret. Now you have seen that he does. You have experienced it, as surely as I did standing on the sidewalk that cold night. And because you now have experienced it, you have an immediate appreciation for the reality of his love. It is no longer simply a part of my reality, about which I share information with you. Now it is a part of your reality. And so you know it in a full, rich, encompassing and effective way.

So why are stories so important to us? They are important because through stories we share not information but experiences, and it is experiences that shape and define our values. It is in the midst of experiences that we have the chance to watch others deal with the challenges of life, to meet new potential heroes. It is through experiences that we have the chance to watch others practice the skills and attitudes and behaviors that make up successful living and to be presented with the invitation to practice those qualities ourselves. It is through experiences that we have the chance to join groups, to observe and encounter their values and to consider making those values our own.

Timothy E. O'Connell, Ph.D.

Yes, it is experiences that shape and define our values, and stories are a second locale for experience. This is the answer the scholars provide.

∞

Through stories we provide experiences to others. That is one of the reasons stories are so important to the human family—and to our individual families, too. But there is another reason. Stories are also important because of what they do for the teller, because of the power that is felt in the experience of storytelling itself.

All of us live our lives in the presence of a reality called "time." That is, our lives have duration, a before and an after. And because this is true, some scholars claim that narrative is the native language for explaining who human beings are.

If I want to explain myself to you, I might try to offer you various words that describe me, words that run the gamut from "compassionate" to "talky," from "thoughtful" to "stubborn." But if I provide you only with those words, your sense of me will remain vague and confusing. Instead, if I really want to explain myself to you, I would do better to tell you the story of my life. I would describe my roots, the parents who gave me life, the settings in which I was reared. I would recount some of the key experiences that shaped me, the steps through which I moved from childhood into adulthood. And in this telling, I would provide you with a focused, textured sense of the reality called Tim O'Connell.

But here is the amazing thing: in so doing I would also give me that same focused, textured understanding. How can that be? The reason is simple but profound. Any good story has a beginning, a middle, and an end, and in crafting a story one must choose each of them. After all, the beginning, for example, is not self-evident. I might start my story with the day of my birth. But might I not do better to start it with the day my parents met? Or perhaps I should begin with the arrival of my great-grandparents on the boat from Ireland. Each of these would provide plausible points of departure. But each of them would give a different tone to my story.

And here is the thrilling truth. When I tell the story of myself, I do not merely recount the facts of my life. Rather, in the very act of telling, I shape those facts. I add to the facts my own interpretation, my sense of their meaning and significance. And thus, the story of my life, obvious though it may be, is also a crafted thing, an artifact that expresses an interpretation of these events through which I have lived and of my moving through and growing out of those experiences that I recount.

Strangely, then, mysteriously, the act of telling my story is an act of birth for me. It is an act through which I provide to me, at the same moment as I provide to you, this focused and textured, interpreted and defined reality called Tim O'Connell. It is in the act of crafting this artifact that is my story that I strangely but truly become the author of myself. I craft myself as surely as I describe myself. And through this act of authoring, I finally claim authority over myself. I own it and embrace it, name it and accept it. I say, "Yes, this is me. With all my foibles and finesse, my beauty and my bestiality, my joy at being victorious and my pain at being vanquished, this is who I am. This, finally, is Tim O'Connell."

<hr />

It has often struck me that every truly mature person that I know has at one time or another made use of the services of a skilled counselor of one kind or another. The counselor may be a professional

Timothy E. O'Connell, Ph.D.

psychotherapist. And as helpful as such experts are to those who are deeply troubled, they are just as helpful to healthy people eager to make fuller sense of the process of their lives. Or the counselor may be a religious leader, a spiritual guide of one kind or another. Or it may even be a wise elder from one's family or community. For this counseling relationship to help, only two things are required.

First, the listener must be skillful. He or she must have the ability to quiet their own issues, to listen with openness and understanding, and to offer in return a summary of what has been heard. And second, the "contract" for the conversation must be that it is one-sided. I want to do the talking, and I want to talk about me. I want to be freed of the usual social responsibility of worrying about how you are taking this and about whether I am providing you enough time to talk about yourself in return. Rather, I want permission to focus on me. And I need to know that this arrangement is alright with you. If these two qualities are there, then the counseling experience can happen.

As I write these words it is spring, and I cannot help observing the college students at the school where I teach. They walk around the campus, hand in hand, starry-eyed with the voltage of new love. And if I eavesdrop just the tiniest bit, I quickly discover the magic of these relationships: They have found someone to whom to tell the story of their lives. They have found this sympathetic listener, someone who will be silent long enough for them to formulate the truths about themselves, someone who will hear and understand and finally affirm the beauty that is revealed. And in the telling and in the listening, these young people are discovering themselves in a new and vital way. No wonder they are in love! No wonder they walk around oblivious to the presence of us lesser mortals, standing mere inches away.

As beautiful as this new love is, however, it is not enough. And you probably know that. Eventually your life becomes more complicated and less clear. Eventually you become enough of a mystery to yourself that the sympathetic listening of your beloved is not enough. Indeed, it may be that your relationship to your beloved is part of the mystery of the moment. At that moment, what do you do? You turn to the more skillful, less entangled listener. You tell the story of your life once more, to this more objective, less invested listener. And what happens then? If you have had this experience, you know the answer already. In this telling to another of your story, you become the author of your life in a new, empowering, affirming way. And as your life's author, you become more fully in charge, less the victim of your life and more the one who shapes and directs. You become more fully alive.

Stories are so important. I tell the story of myself, thereby defining and understanding myself. I see the values that have characterized my life. Some of those values I affirm. I notice the times I have been honest and kind. I declare to myself that I am an honest person. And the result is that I am an honest person more truly and more firmly than before. These values are confirmed. At the same time, some of the values are rejected. I notice the times I have been selfish and indulgent. In looking straightforwardly at these experiences and naming clearly for myself the values they reflect, I decide that this is not who I want to be. And so I recommit myself to living other values, and thereby I stimulate growth and change in my life. Different values are confirmed.

And stories are yet more important. I tell the story of myself, thereby sharing with you the experiences that are mine. I give you those experiences, activating them through the movie projector of your mind, so that the values that were manifest to me may be manifest as well to you. You, too, see those values, observe them and taste them and feel them. You, too, embrace some and reject others. You, too, feel the impetus to growth and change. In you, as in me, values are, one way or another, confirmed.

And stories are more important still. I tell the stories of those who have gone before, of the people and events that have shaped us and made us who we are. I tell the crafted stories that carry the values that I cherish, the "fictions" that are profoundly true, if only in another way.

That is what I do. And that is what I recommend to you.

Do you want to pass on values to your children? Tell stories. Tell stories of yourself. Tell stories of the experiences you have had. Tell stories of the people you have met. Tell stories of those who have gone before, even if you yourself know these forebears only through the stories that you have heard. Tell the stories that are important to you, having been told to you in important moments of your life. Tell stories, and then tell them again.

When the children declare, "Tell me a story," hear it as a sacred command. For their request is not for an evening of entertainment. Their request is for a key to life.

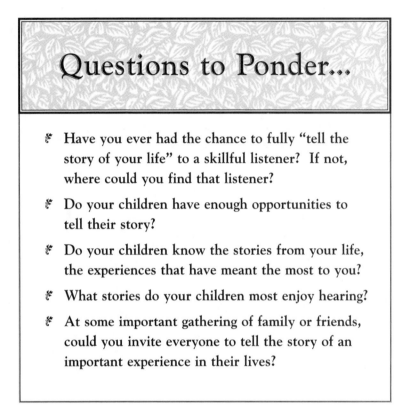

Questions to Ponder...

❦ Have you ever had the chance to fully "tell the story of your life" to a skillful listener? If not, where could you find that listener?

❦ Do your children have enough opportunities to tell their story?

❦ Do your children know the stories from your life, the experiences that have meant the most to you?

❦ What stories do your children most enjoy hearing?

❦ At some important gathering of family or friends, could you invite everyone to tell the story of an important experience in their lives?

7

Stories of our Lives

And then there are the great stories, used by great groups to pass on the great values that are at the center of our lives and our civilization. For, as we have seen, the native habitat of values is groups. And, as we have also seen, values are passed along not just by the external experiences of our everyday lives but also by the imaginative experiences that take place through the stories we are told. But if both these ideas are true, you will not be surprised to learn that groups use stories in a most special way, to pass on the values for which they stand.

Most especially is this true of religious groups.

Every Christmas I watch parents walk their children to the crib. I eavesdrop as they tell the story once again of Baby Jesus, of his mother Mary, of the shepherds and the wise men and, yes, of the donkey that stands mute, in loving adoration. They tell the story of that great night, of the wonder it expressed and the gift it brought.

For other Christians the story that catches it all is the story of the cross, the old rugged cross. They tell their children the story of that frightful but graceful day, of the faithfulness of Jesus, of the betrayal of the followers, of the patient presence of the women.

They tell the story of that "wondrous love" that showed itself as it hung upon the cross.

Jewish families gather around the solemn table of the Passover dinner. And the youngest stands up, bold but a bit stagestruck. And again, in an annual ritual, the question is asked, "Father, why is this night different than other nights?" And the story is told once again. The fear of the Israelites, the courage of Moses, the anger of the Egyptians, and finally the power of God.

And the same thing happens with Muslims, Hindus, Buddhists, and all the adherents of the other great religions. I will not attempt to describe their stories because I do not know them well enough. These are not my stories, and I would dishonor them by trying some sort of second-hand summary. But I know these stories exist. And I know that, for these people as for my people, the stories carry the central values of the group and that, for them as for me, the group transmits its values by repeating in endless cycle the stories that are the center of its life.

This is what a wonderful scholar, Stanley Hauerwas, meant when he said that churches are "story formed communities." And this is what challenges us to be faithful to our religious communities. And to tell their stories ourselves.

∞

I am amazed how often my friends, who would describe themselves as ordinary people, hold back from telling these powerful religious stories. I suppose they feel they don't know them well enough. But they do.

I love to perform a little experiment, in which I ask people to describe the scene of a religious story from their own tradition. For example, I will ask Christians if they recall the story of Zacchaeus, the short man who climbed a tree to get a look at Jesus. And then I ask: "From the point of view of Jesus, as he is walking down the road, is that tree on the left or the right?" And the amazing thing: My listeners have an answer!

Of course, the biblical story does not tell us which side the tree is on. The point is that for years people have been picturing these stories as they heard them, with the result that their imaginations have quite detailed pictures of the scene. They know the story quite well, whether they realize it or not.

I discovered the same thing when I was asked, for a particular occasion, to memorize a biblical story and proclaim it without a text. I was frightened by the request. I am not, in general, very good at memorizing things. But when I sat down to attempt the task, I was astonished to discover that it wasn't very hard at all. I already knew the story, after all. The process of memorizing was little more than a process of tidying up the details of word order.

When we're telling stories to children, details of word order are unimportant. Just tell the story! And if you're going to seek to pass on your values by telling any stories at all, by all means pass on your most important values by telling your children the stories of your religion, the stories that, quite literally, define the world you inhabit.

That is what happens when religious teachers share stories with the children. Have you sent your children to a summer bible camp? Do you arrange for them to have religious instruction? In such settings it may irritate you if you find out the teacher is "wasting time" just telling stories. But I hope you can now see that this activity isn't wasting time at all. In fact, it is in many ways the central activity of the process of religious education.

Timothy E. O'Connell, Ph.D.

Religious leaders are coming to understand this. They are realizing that good preaching is less a matter of careful intellectual analysis and more a matter of imaginative story-telling. When I was a freshman in high school, our school required us to participate in a three-day retreat, a time of prayer and reflection. And the days were led by a clergyman, who was to inspire us by his preaching. This particular clergyman, a young man, was wise beyond his years in knowing the path to the hearts of young people. In the formal sessions of three full days, he did nothing but tell stories, one right after another. Some were the traditional stories of our religious heritage. Some were fantastic products of his own imagination.

This was forty years ago. But I can still remember the story of Joey, riding the bus home from school, who suddenly sees the devil get on the bus, bringing a temptation to sin. Joey knows he's no match for the devil, and fears that all is lost. But then, suddenly, Joey recalls being told that even the briefest of prayers can mobilize all the power of heaven. So he whispers a prayer to his Lord, "Jesus, help me." He asks for the help of those who have gone before, "Mary and all the saints, intercede for me." And hearing these words, the devil screams, covering his ears. And at the next stop, the devil flees the bus, no match for the team of Joey, his friends, and his God.

Yes, I can see it still, after forty years. That is the power of stories.

$$\infty$$

Ah, the stories of our people, how they define and illumine who we are. And among these sources of our "peoplehood," religion is not alone. Think also of ethnic and national groups, and the stories that they recount. Last year I saw the movie rendition of the life of Irish patriot Michael Collins. I confess that I'm a rather completely

Tend Your Own Garden

Americanized Irishman, so the story was new to me. I found it interesting, even moving, but I didn't really feel like it was my story. And then, as I was leaving the movie theater, I came upon a woman who works in my department. She and her husband were also leaving the theater. I noticed right away her red eyes and somber face. "Wasn't that beautiful," she said. "Such a great man, such a great man!" I asked her, in my foolishness, if she had known the story of Michael Collins. "Oh, of course," she replied, "we have a picture of him hanging in our home." Her parting words, wise woman that she was, announced that "I have to be sure all the children see this movie, for sure!"

The many ethnic groups that comprise America all have their stories. And no matter how much we may also be one people, these stories remain important to us. The book, *Roots*, and the television movie made from it, is a wonderful example. The characters within the story took on meaning as the path of their lives was traced through succeeding generations. And millions of African Americans, in reading the book and watching the movie, had the chance to discern their own story, so often overlooked, actually ignored, in our society. They had the chance to know who they were, a learning that is critical to all human persons.

And what about you? Are there stories of your people that you cherish, stories of your national roots and of the heroes who led the way? And do you tell those stories to your children, to the next generation that shares your lineage and heritage? I hope so.

Finally, we must consider the stories of our common American heritage. How often visitors from other lands want to try to grasp what is different about Americans. We can put out lots of words on our difference, abstract words of many kinds. And the words may be true, but I doubt that they will convey the real truth of who we are. Rather, we do better at explaining ourselves when we tell our stories.

Timothy E. O'Connell, Ph.D.

We recall the Boston Tea Party and the War of Independence. We talk of George Washington and Thomas Jefferson, recalling their features, recounting their words, even describing their homes. We speak of Abraham Lincoln, of the bloody War Between the States, and of the struggle to bring freedom to those enslaved. And we acknowledge some of the painful differences among us when we discover the different ways this story is told, even a century later, by different citizens. We tell the story of the struggle against Nazi and Fascist pretensions, and we speak with pride. We tell the story of the struggle against revolutionary forces in Vietnam, and we speak with . . . what? With shame? With embarrassment? With anger? It all depends on the story that we tell.

But tell the stories, we do. And in the telling we express the values that we cherish. And in the expressing we also transmit those values, presenting them to the imaginations of those who listen, eliciting in them the experience that can change their values as well.

∞

I love the movie *Resurrection*. The movie tells the story of a woman, Edna Mae, who, driving with her husband, is involved in a car crash. He is killed, and she needs to be revived after her heart briefly stops. During those moments, she tells us, she had a "near-death experience," which moved and touched her deeply. Then, in the months following, she slowly, accidentally discovers in herself a new capability: She can heal people.

Needless to say, this attracts lots of attention, but much of it is negative. Some people claim she's a fake. Others, speaking for institutionalized religion, ask why she doesn't include more explicit prayer. And yet others, caught in their own personal ambivalence, can't stand to have her around. To all of them she replies with her simple truth: "I don't know how it works. I love them and they get better."

I know that this brief synopsis cannot convey of the power of this movie. I recount this tiny summary only to tell you something of myself. For the truth is that this movie changed me and that, in the years since I first saw it, Edna Mae's simple explanation has been a key for me to what's really important in life: We love, and things get better in the end.

I was similarly moved when, as a college student, I read John Steinbeck's novel, *Of Mice and Men*. It tells the story of two cowboys, George and his rather dim-witted friend, Lenny. Lenny, not fully appreciating his own strength, has accidentally killed the woman he loves. In his simplicity, Lenny is terrified of being locked in small places, and a jail would be pure pain for him. So George and Lenny are fleeing. As the posse closes in, George struggles with his dilemma: how to protect Lenny in this hopeless situation. At the last minute, rather than inflict on Lenny a future of pain he cannot understand, George kills him.

I remember so clearly my reading of this book; I know the room I was in and the time of day when I finished it. And I know that it changed me forever. It would be too simple for me to say that I think George was "right" in what he did. I suppose that, in the end, I would say he was wrong. But the lesson of the book for me wasn't about right and wrong; it was about how complicated life is. In reading the book, I felt that complication to the center of my soul. And in the years since then, I have never forgotten it.

If *Resurrection* and *Of Mice and Men* have touched me this way, I'd wager that some other tale has had a similar effect on you. It may be a movie or a novel, a television show or an opera, a stage play or a musical. But for most of us, there are works of art that touch us and change us in ways that are hard to explain.

And if you think about it, this power of literature to shape our soul is amazing. After all, they are "fictions," they tell things that never happened. But of course, that's not quite accurate. Through the artistry of their creators, these stories make contact with profound truths, truths that "ring true" as we read them, truths that, once noticed, can never again be ignored. Indeed, that is the function of the artist in our world. Artists are people who have a profound sense of what is really true about life and who have the rare ability to show it to us rather than just tell us about it.

And from time immemorial artists have been doing this. The group gathered around that ancient bonfire received not only stories of their past. They also relished obviously made-up stories that caught deeper truths in the fabric of the lives they described. They enjoyed the blessing of an artist's wise creation. And societies of that sort knew so well how important these stories were that they honored these storytellers as special members of the community's elite.

Over the centuries, this role of storyteller has never been lost, though it has taken on varied shapes. Often they were members of the clergy, or exercised their craft in religious settings. The medieval morality plays, performed on the front steps of Europe's cathedrals, for example, or the great Greek tragedies, enacted in the amphitheater. And in later times theaters, from Shakespeare's Globe to the Paris Opera House to New York's Palace Theater to the Hollywood Bowl, served the same function, providing a setting in which we can receive and enjoy the sad and funny, ever-beautiful "stories of our lives." But consistently, stories and the craft of storytelling have been a hallmark of human civilization.

Tend Your Own Garden

Today the storytelling tradition continues. But there are new problems in our time, the result of the tremendous power of television. And those of us who wish to pass on important values, and who realize the power of stories, must be aware of these problems.

For one thing, television has brought about the most centralized structure for storytelling that the world has ever seen. Our whole society is dependent upon a smaller number of storytellers than at any moment in history. And those storytellers have more power than any others who have ever lived. For another thing, given the commercial nature of television, we can't help being terribly suspicious of the motives of these storytellers. Of course, artists have always had to please their patrons, and prostituting one's art to commercial realities is hardly new. But the problem is certainly intensified for us, with our painful awareness of the ways in which advertising shapes and determines the stories that we receive.

And then, as if all this were not enough of a problem, the mechanics of television mean that we tend to watch shows from the isolation of our living rooms. For most of history, storytelling and story listening have occurred in a group setting. As we were in the presence of the story, we were also in one another's presence. And along with the direct communication from the storyteller or the actors to ourselves, there was also a non-stop flow of lateral communication in which we let one another know how the story was striking us. We laughed at the same jokes—or we didn't. We were moved by the same developments—or we weren't. We were horrified by the same dramatic actions—or we were pleased. Not only did we talk about the story afterward, we communicated to one another our reactions to it in the very midst of the experience.

That is often not the case any more. Now, at the very moment when I am connected to this all-powerful storyteller, I am also cut off from my colleagues in the audience. Is that joke really funny, or is it vulgar? The reaction of the studio audience or the laugh track is my only clue. Does that story, frightening though it may be, catch an important life-truth or does it, in some serious way, lie about the reality it portrays? I must rely on my own isolated judgment, and that is not enough.

I point this out not to invite you to despair. Actually there is a lot we can do to resist this state of affairs, and many people are doing it already. Most important, we talk about what we see. Around water coolers in offices, in the parking lots next to schools, on the front steps of churches and mosques and synagogues, people talk about the shows they have seen. I want to applaud this activity. And I hope to alert you to how important it is.

Beyond that, we could even go so far as to make efforts to watch television in groups. People gather in groups to watch football games, after all. I recall one Sunday afternoon when I was changing airplanes in Denver, Colorado. I am only a modest football fan, and Denver is not my city. It never occurred to me how much a game that involves the Denver Broncos is a civic event! But there they were, up and down the concourse: groups huddled around television sets. At one point the Broncos scored, and the cheer rolled around that massive building like a surfer's wave heading for the beach that never comes. Would that we could make our viewing more consistently such a community thing.

Tend Your Own Garden

The stories of our lives come in many forms. They exist in the life-defining stories of our religious traditions. They arise in the identity-forming stories of our ethnic heritages and our national roots. They appear in the truth-revealing stories that skillful, faithful artists craft as their gift to us all. And in all these forms they nourish our spirits, warm our hearts, and shape our values.

So here is the lesson. Respect the stories you have received. Pass those stories on, telling them to those you love. Bring yourself and your own to the best of the new stories that come your way. Remember the power of stories, and handle them carefully, testing them against the wisdom of the communities where you live.

And when the spirit moves, make your own contribution. Close your eyes, describe what you see, give life to the characters of your imagination, trust them as they take flight and become strangely free, and tell those you love the story in your heart.

For it is, never doubt, the story of our lives.

Timothy E. O'Connell, Ph.D.

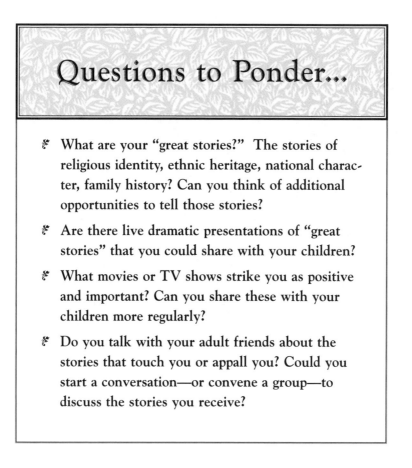

Questions to Ponder...

- ✼ What are your "great stories?" The stories of religious identity, ethnic heritage, national character, family history? Can you think of additional opportunities to tell those stories?

- ✼ Are there live dramatic presentations of "great stories" that you could share with your children?

- ✼ What movies or TV shows strike you as positive and important? Can you share these with your children more regularly?

- ✼ Do you talk with your adult friends about the stories that touch you or appall you? Could you start a conversation—or convene a group—to discuss the stories you receive?

8

Body Language

One of my good friends in college was a fellow with a long Polish name. At first, I found it hard to spell his name; and like many of my classmates, I took pride when I finally mastered its intricacies. I even learned to speak the name not only in its adjusted, Americanized version, but also in its correct Polish pronunciation. The funny thing was that, in all this ethnic attention, my classmates and I seemed more intrigued with my friend's Polish identity than he did. He, on the contrary, seemed to see himself as an "ordinary American."

But then he got married. The woman he married was, indeed, a rather typical American, both in her name and in her interests. So at first the lifestyle of their marriage was a straightforward reflection of the American customs we encounter on TV. When his wife became pregnant, however, something began to change. All of a sudden my friend altered his priorities; he asked his wife to pay a visit to his mother and ask for her culinary assistance.

And I don't mean just good cooking. My friend explained to his wife, and later to all of us, that while he didn't usually make too much of his Polish heritage, he actually had a deep affection for the customs of his forebears. And now that he was going to have children, he didn't want those traditions to die out. So he was asking his Anglo-Saxon wife to go to his deeply Polish mother to learn the recipes for the traditional feasts, most particularly for the fish dinner of Christmas Eve and the beautiful rituals of reconciliation that accompany it.

"I don't want my kids to grow up in a bland and colorless home," he said. "I want them to have the rich childhood memories that I enjoy, the wonderful sense of doing something that our family has been doing for centuries."

We human beings are communicating animals. We always seem to be either telling something to the people around us, or receiving the communications that they are sending our way. Actually, I suppose we're always doing both. That's what the magical chemistry between storyteller and audience is all about.

But the truth is that we humans have two languages with which to communicate, not one. We don't only have words, we also have gestures. We have not only the word "hello," we also have the wave and the handshake. We have not only the declaration "I love you," we also have the kiss and the smile and the look that speaks volumes all at once. Yes, we have two languages. Body language is, paradoxically, a body's other language.

In fact, it's probably more accurate to say that body language is a body's first language. The baby communicates long before it learns to use words. And people traveling in foreign countries often succeed in communicating without the aid of any of the local language. So the language of gesture seems to be more central, more original to being human than is the language of verbal communication.

Tend Your Own Garden

This is an important idea. After all, we are interested in passing along the values that shape and enrich our lives. But how shall we do that? We've seen that one of the ways is by that communication through which we touch the imaginations of others, allowing them to enter into experiences that can change them. For that communication, we've said, we use the beautiful poetry of storytelling. But now I want to add this other point. We pass along our values by the poetic communication of word and gesture. Or maybe more accurately, we pass along our values through the stories that show those values to the imagination of others and through the gestures that manifest those values in ourselves.

One of the mysteries of being human is that it's rather hard to tell a lie. We humans seem to be designed for truth. Of course, we can lie, we can use words to deceive our listeners, but it takes work. And it never altogether succeeds. When our verbal language becomes false, our body language rebels. Our blood pressure jumps a bit, our pulse accelerates, our palms sweat, small electrical impulses communicate the body language's protest against the deception that is going on. And this is what the lie detector machine notices and measures.

This is what we human persons notice, too. You ask your child, "Johnny, did you break that window?" A tidal wave of words comes back, a great array of explanations. But you can feel, between the lines of all the words, in the evasive eyes and the frantic body, the truth that is not yet spoken. Dear child that he is, he just doesn't know how to lie. And even with adults, with people who, sad to say, have become much better at lying, we can often feel the distracting, shifty gestures that betray the deeper truth. And we declare, "I'm not sure what's going on, but I just feel like he or she is lying."

Timothy E. O'Connell, Ph.D.

I remember watching a religious leader on television, a man for zhis followers. Something seemed not right. And then it struck me: His eyes were never on the person he was touching, the person with whom he was talking. Instead, his eyes were always out ahead, scanning the crowd, looking for the next contact. And I was saddened. I don't doubt that he is a good man who does much good work. But I was disappointed to know that he was not being really, genuinely truthful in this moment. His words may have offered personal greeting, but his body revealed that he was somewhere else altogether. And so, in a small but undeniable sense, his words were telling a lie.

Now, here is the saddest truth of all: If we really work at it, we humans can even learn to lie with our bodies. We can offer the handclasp of friendship to someone we really despise. We can laugh at the joke we find offensive. We can kiss the person we no longer love. We can applaud the leader we hope to depose. And yes, we can achieve sexual intimacy with the partner we would just as soon put to death.

How repulsive we find that kind of duplicity. And you can see now why it is so ugly. This kind of lying is a kind of ultimate insult against the meaning of the human person. It is a sort of radical contradiction of who we are and who we want to be. When we take the body's first language, our first and foremost tool of true communication, and make it instead a tool of deception, we attack our honor at its most central place. In fact, when our bodies learn to lie, I'm not sure how we ever recover our truthfulness. For there is no deeper language to set the body straight. Oh, we can try to use words to make us aware, just as I am doing here. But there is no guarantee it will work. A lying body is a dangerous thing.

Tend Your Own Garden

On the other hand, give the body a chance to take the lead, and our words and our hearts will follow soon enough. I once heard a college student announce: "I can't have sex with the same girl more than a couple of times. I've found that if you stay too long, you begin to care about her!" The comment is pathetic and enraging. But it also contains a weird bit of truth. Where the body leads, the heart will surely follow. Ideally we should be intimate only with those we love, to whom we are committed. But it does work the other way, as well. Be intimate with a person often enough, and you will find you are becoming committed. Your body won't let it be any other way.

So there is something to be said for shaking hands with the person you sometimes oppose. At the same moment that the gesture bespeaks fellowship, it can also help it come about. There is something to be said for rising to your feet for the leader you don't always admire. Your honoring of the office will help you see more clearly the complexity of the person. There is something to be said for kissing goodnight, even in the presence of a conflict not altogether resolved. As the kiss should express unity, it can also help it return.

Back in the 1960s, the Roman Catholic Church revised many of its ceremonies. And in the case of its ordinary Sunday worship, the church added a small moment of gesture, a time when the participants were to exchange a handshake of peace and fellowship. I remember that time, and how awkward, even wrong that gesture felt. I had been raised in a religion that said we go to church to be alone with God. The other people around me are irrelevant, perhaps even distractions from the only important thing. And so this act of turning toward my neighbor felt altogether wrong.

Timothy E. O'Connell, Ph.D.

But like many members of my church, I trustingly cooperated with the change my leaders proposed. And slowly, but inevitably, my understandings began to shift. Compared to the power of body language, my ideas didn't stand a chance! Little by little I came to understand that God and neighbor are not enemies, that love of neighbor is the way I express love of God and that, when we go to God, we go together.

Yes, the language of the body is a powerful thing. Because of that, it ought to be used intentionally, to express what we really intend.

I have a friend who enacts a wonderful custom at the beginning of any shared meal. We may be sitting in a quite elegant restaurant, dressed in our high-style finery. There may be a cocktail resting before each of our places. The scene may feel completely spontaneous, without any structure whatsoever. But then my friend will act. Quietly, he reaches into the bread basket, takes out a roll, and holds it out to me. I try to take it, but he does not let go. Then I realize: I am to hold the other side, tearing the roll between us. We break bread in this way, silently and with no additional ceremony. And then the general conversation resumes.

I love this gesture of his, and I am touched whenever it occurs. I am aware, of course, how "breaking bread" is a part of many ancient religious traditions, how Jews cherish its message of Passover salvation, how Muslims use it to seal the sacrifice of Ramadan, how Christians believe it is the setting for the most intimate experience of God's love. But there is something more. I think now that this gesture of my friend's is the source and that those religious rituals are the extension, not the other way around. I think what he does with me in this restaurant is not important primarily because it refers to religious convictions that are important to us both. Rather, I think

96

that in this primitive human gesture of his I am experiencing the reason why those formal ceremonies are so right, so true, and so important to all who believe.

∞

I want to call for an examination of body-conscience. Many religious traditions call for a periodic examination of conscience. I want to call for a particular sort. Look at your gestures, and consider the message they speak. You may not like the idea, but the fact is that the message of your gestures probably reveals the true character of the values that define your life.

When I was a young adult, I had occasion to visit the home of some distant relatives. I had met a few members of that family, and I was fond of them. So I looked forward to visiting their home. But then came dinner. The husband and the sons sat at the table. And I, of course, was invited to join them. The daughters occupied their seats part of the time, though they also jumped up periodically to get some food, clear the plates, and such. And the wife? She never did sit down. Through the whole meal she commuted between kitchen and dining room, seeing to the comfort of everyone else.

I was deeply disturbed by this experience. I don't know how conscious this family was of the values expressed by their domestic gestures. But to me, an outsider, they screamed at a painful pitch. The inequity they proclaimed, the two-tiered world they supposed, the lack of regard they implied, were awful to observe. And I felt guilty at the complicity of my presence at this table of disunion.

What about the gestures and rituals of your home? Do they say what you wish to mean? Do you run into the house without a kiss for your spouse, a hug for your children? Do you clean up after yourself, or leave a mess wherever you walk? Do you listen when others are speaking, or do you sort through the mail while the conversation proceeds? Is the newspaper a source of information, or an Iron Curtain of intra-family politics? Look at your gestures. And if they don't express the values you want, how can you change them, so that they in turn can change the way you think?

Look also at your place of work. What is the message revealed by the body language there? How is the office arranged? Where do people sit at the meetings? What is the structure of the arrangements for meals, for parking, even for lavatory breaks?

I know of a Midwestern company that built, at great expense, a new corporate headquarters. The set of buildings was an architectural marvel, several independent structures connected by futuristic glass-enclosed overpasses. When the employees moved into these buildings, they were assigned in a way that seemed to make sense, that was designed for maximum efficiency. And as one element of this apparently sensible plan, all of the top administrators were placed in close proximity to each other, in one of the individual buildings.

Then the talk began. Soon the common joke of employees was to refer to this administration building as "the castle." The overpass leading to it was "the bridge." And the space beneath the bridge was, of course, "the moat." "Did you hear the rumor? Our profits for last quarter were so bad, the boss is going to pull up the bridge, shut off the heat and let us freeze to death. He's never coming out of the castle again!"

The story has a happy ending, I'm glad to say. Eventually the managers realized the negative body language of the arrangement they were using, and they changed it. They redistributed the offices of top administrators to a variety of locations around the corporate campus.

Tend Your Own Garden

They structured office activities in such a way that travel between buildings was maximized. And soon there appeared a new generation of employees who knew nothing of the castle, the bridge, and the moat.

The same thing can happen in the place of work that you influence, if you examine your conscience about the language your gestures implies.

Look at the gestures of your own personal style. Do you pump the accelerator of your car, pushing for any advantage, cutting off the laggard who leaves the tiniest space ahead? Do you run into church or synagogue or mosque a few minutes late and escape before the ceremony is concluded? What clothes do you wear? Are you always in uniform, whether the uniform is a military tunic or a grey flannel suit or a house dress? Does your name always appear with its title, whether the title is Reverend or Mom? What does it mean that you always wear those sunglasses, the kind with the silver coating? In a word, what is the message of your own nonverbal proclamations?

These questions are not simple, of course. I have heard young clergy argue that they should never be in uniform. They believe the vesture isolates them from other people. Actually, I think, the real issue is that they are not yet comfortable with the inner identity of the profession they have entered. Just as I would want to argue that one should abandon the uniform when off-duty, so I would argue that one should wear it when work is going on.

No, it's not simple. But it is important. Look at your body language. If these are your gestures, these are probably your values. And at the very least, you had better come to realize what your values really are. After all, lying to yourself is the worst thing of all. So examine your body-conscience. And then make changes, where changes ought to happen.

Timothy E. O'Connell, Ph.D.

And expect it to hurt a little bit! I have talked about how uncomfortable I felt when I began the practice of greeting my neighbor in church. Whenever we attempt new gestures, some discomfort is inevitable. If it has not been my way to express affection through physical touch, it will take some work to develop ease. If it has been my tendency to hide behind my titles and office, it will require effort to strip away this facade.

But the effort is important, for the stakes are high. A woman friend of mine once told me of the time she took a group of children to the zoo. This zoo had a petting area, where the children could touch and hold the animals. And today's animal? A snake! My friend was afraid of snakes. But, as she told me, she petted it just the same. "I don't want the kids to grow up with my fears. I don't want to pass that on!"

May these words be ours as well. Let's check our body language for truth, for what we believe right now. And then check it for wish, for what we want to believe and proclaim. On the basis of this reflection, then, let's do what needs to be done.

Let's make sure the values of our body's first language, the language of gesture and ritual, are the values we want to pass on. For never doubt, they are the values the children will learn. They are the values we will give them, no matter what cheap talk may claim.

Questions to Ponder...

- Do your gestures express what you feel? What you believe?

- What gestures do you wish felt more comfortable? What can you do to practice them?

- What are the rituals of your family? Would you like to change or develop them? How might you do that?

- In the various areas of your life, what rituals do you most cherish? Do you enact them often? Are you passing them on to your children?

- What rituals of respect should your children show? Can you teach those rituals—explaining them clearly—and call for them?

9

Tend Your Own Garden

In 1972, I was living in New York City, completing studies on my doctoral degree. My focus was Christian ethics, with special attention to the basic ideas that shape that field: What is right and wrong? How can human persons live freely and responsibly? I needed a break from the work, and set out to see a Broadway show. The show was *Candide*, a musical composed by Leonard Bernstein.

Based on an old tale, the show tells of Candide and his beloved Cunegonde who have been taught by their teacher, the silly philosopher, Dr. Pangloss, that they live in the best of all possible worlds. Our heroes undergo the most outrageous (and hilarious) misfortunes. They are shipwrecked, attacked by heathens, sold into slavery, and sentenced to death for heresy. But throughout, Candide and Cunegonde keep insisting that these difficulties must merely be apparent. After all, they live in the best of all possible worlds. Therefore, everything must be happening for the best, whether they can recognize this or not.

Finally, their disasters become just too horrendous to deny, and they decide to forsake silly illusions in favor of honest and loving ways. They achieve real wisdom. Thus the comedy ends on a serious note. The final song, set to glorious music, allows Candide and Cunegonde to proclaim their hard-won insight.

> Let dreamers dream what worlds they please;
> Those Edens can't be found;
> The sweetest flow'rs, the fairest trees
> Are grown in solid ground.
>
> We're neither pure nor wise nor good;
> We'll do the best we know;
> We'll build our house, and chop our wood,
> And make our garden grow,
> And make our garden grow.

I became a gardener late in life, and almost by accident. A trip to the hardware store in late November led me past the clearance counter, where the last tulip bulbs were on sale. I was not a person who could keep anything growing, but I had the urge to take a risk. At least the bargain price was right! So I bought the bulbs and shoved them in the ground. And then I forgot about them.

But then spring arrived. What are those tiny green shoots coming out of the soil? Who put those there? My tulips! They are alive. They have grown. And they have produced the most beautiful flowers in the history of the world (or so it seemed to me).

The experience was a conversion for me. I loved the beauty that my effort produced, so I have never stopped gardening. Over the succeeding years I have lived in three different homes, but in each of them I have started a garden. Now, from April to November my fingers are never completely free of dirt, as I serve my perennial garden, my annual flowers, my vegetables. I greet my garden in the morning, and I often look at it last thing at night. I rejoice when it is blessed by a gentle spring rain. And when violent storms threaten it, I respond protectively, with stakes and wire and string. I take care of my garden, and in return it blesses me with beauty.

Yes, I love the beauty that my gardening produces. But I also love the magic of a growth I have never completely understood and that I have never really owned. For the process is, after all, mysterious and amazing and humbling, all at the same time. I don't know why these plants grow. And even as I enjoy all this beauty, I never really control it.

But I have learned a few things. On the one hand, I have learned that plants want to grow. Most plants, given basic care and reasonable attention, do succeed in growing. And the reason is not the talent of the gardener. It is their own inner dynamism, their radical, central inclination to grow, given the chance. On the other hand, I have learned that dangers lurk, that pests can suck life out of these plants, that forces too strong can overwhelm them. And so sometimes, despite my best efforts and in the face of what appears a completely good situation, they simply do not survive. So my gardening is, in the end, a mysterious and unpredictable thing.

The same is true for the gardens of our lives, where we seek to cultivate in those we love a genuinely good way of life. I believe all the insights I have shared in these pages. My experience teaches me, and the wisdom of those from whom I've learned confirms, that these suggestions make it much more likely that our values will live on after us. But there is no guarantee. The center of our children is as mysterious as any garden flower. On the one hand, they too have an inner drive to grow. On the other hand, they too are subject to dangers we cannot always see and that we will not ever control.

This is not, I realize, particularly good news. In the first pages of this book I told you of the man I saw in a diner, spending a lunch with the little daughter he loved. I feel sad that I must tell him, in the end, that there is no guarantee. I regret that, after all my suggestions, success is never assured. But that is the truth. And if this truth is not altogether pleasant, it is still preferable to the foolish falsehoods of Dr. Pangloss and his compatriots.

There are no guarantees when it comes to passing on our values to our children. But there is a strategy, a truth we can count on. Do you want to pass on your cherished values to your children? Then, tend your garden and make your garden grow.

Tend your own garden. Children don't listen, they observe. They want to see how we live our own lives. So the most important thing we can do, to assure that our children will grow up honest and true, compassionate and fair, is to work at living those values ourselves. It can't be faked, it can't be disguised. It can simply be pursued with integrity and effort. Let the conduct of your own life be a model that your children can observe and imitate. Be a hero to them. And put your children in contact with other heros, admirable people who can also give them images of a possible way of life.

Tend your own garden. Children are born into groups, and in groups they grow or die. Create groups that live the values you embrace, defend those groups and support them with your care. The group of your family, of course, but other groups as well. Your children's groups: playmates, neighbors, school chums, sports partners.

Tend Your Own Garden

And also grown-up groups: extended family, church groups, fellow-ships of prayer and service, social groups of good will and gentleness. It's sometimes awfully hard, of course. We are never far from groups that we despise, that threaten to undermine our commitments and frustrate our dreams for our children. But as Candide discovered, the fact that it's hard doesn't make it any less true. In this world, which at times is certainly not the best of all possible worlds, people behave like the groups they belong to.

Tend your own garden. Practice makes permanent, after all. So enact your values. Do deeds of goodness, allowing the smallest gestures to deepen the convictions you propose. And insist that your children do the same. As tough as it is to remember—and to live, face the truth that the person of tomorrow is created by the tiny actions of today. When the two-year-old is required to give back the toy she has taken, a woman of honesty is coming to birth. When the six-year-old is encouraged to face the lie he has spoken, a man of truthfulness is growing taller before our eyes. When our children are challenged to say "thank you" and "please" and "if I may," adults of kindness and sensitivity are learning how to act—and who to be.

Tend your own garden. Fill the imaginations of your children with stories of honor and of beauty. Stories of struggle, too, of difficulties and even of failure. But stories of hope and inspiration. Tell the stories of your parents, and of the heroes of your past. Tell the stories of your world, and of the heroes of your time. Tell the great stories of all people, the stories of faith and vision. Tell stories of God and stories of the world. Tell the stories that were told to you. And tell the stories that artists make, the stories you have read and heard and seen, the stories that have touched you and spoken to you a truth that offers life.

Timothy E. O'Connell, Ph.D.

Tend your own garden. Dance the truths you believe in the gestures and rituals of your life, in the thank-you notes and returned phone calls, in the hugs and kisses, in the family dinners and weekly worships and community involvements. Take seriously the gestures of your religious tradition, the bows and genuflections, the looks and touches, the eatings and drinkings, the vestures and groomings of your faith. Never underestimate their ability to speak. Look for new ways to symbolically enact your values, constructing gestures of care and commitment, of faith and fidelity, of gentleness and support. And let the love that exists among you have regular release in appropriate gestures, from the sexual sharing of spouses to the pats and clasps of relatives and friends.

Yes, tend your own garden. It will not guarantee growth, this I must admit. But only there will true growth take place, this I know most surely.

Tend your own garden. That is my final message to that wonderful man who shared a lunch with his adorable, giggling daughter.

And it is my final message to you.

Tend Your Own Garden

Candide:

You've been a fool and so have I,
But come and be my wife.
And let us try before we die
To make some sense of life.

Cunegonde:

I thought the world was sugar cake,
For so our master said;
But now I'll teach my hands to bake
Our loaf of daily bread.

Both:

Let dreamers dream what worlds they please;
Those Edens can't be found;
The sweetest flow'rs, the fairest trees
Are grown in solid ground.

All:

We're neither pure nor wise nor good;
We'll do the best we know;
We'll build our house, and chop our wood,
And make our garden grow,
And make our garden grow.

109

Questions to Ponder...

❦ What foolishness, a la Dr. Pangloss, gets in the way of growing your garden? What can you do to free yourself from it?

❦ What corner of your garden most needs tending? What one initiative would most achieve that goal?

❦ What action of your children would stimulate the garden of their values? How can you encourage that action?

❦ Do you know anyone else who would benefit from the ideas you have encountered here? How can you share the ideas, so that yet another garden may grow?

"An insightful and practical book for parents and anyone involved with children!"

"In his timely book, *Tend Your Own Garden*, Timothy O'Connell leads us through his experiences and observations, to the ultimate truth and challenge that the transmission of morals and values to our children begins at home. He reminds us that our daily parental example leaves a formative mark on our children. He provides pragmatic ideas that inspire us to raise good kids while recognizing it is not easy but it is a worthwhile and attainable goal. This is an insightful and practical book for parents and anyone involved with children!"

> — **Catherine Musco Garcia-Prats and Joseph A. Garcia-Prats, M.D.**, authors of the best-seller *Good Families Don't Just Happen: What We Learned from Raising our 10 Sons and How It Can Work for You*

"In my work with families, *Tend Your Own Garden* will encourage me to stress even more profoundly the role of story and the value of togetherness in families. This will make parents look honestly at what they are trying to give to their children. And this honesty, in turn, will lead them to re-evaluate their approach to parenting."

> — **Bill Elliott, OMI**
> Pastor of Our Lady of Guadalupe Church, Austin, Texas

"Tim challenges us to be the sort of persons we claim to be . . . Great book for parents, grandparents, teachers, and all those who interact with children and families!"

> — **Judy Clark, M.Accd, M.Ed., L.P.C.,** past president of the National Association of Catholic Family Life Ministers

Timothy E. O'Connell, Ph.D.

TIMOTHY O'CONNELL, PH.D., is a professor of pastoral studies at Loyola University in Chicago. A widely known author and speaker, Dr. O'Connell has written eight books and numerous articles. *Tend Your Own Garden* is the first of a series of books by Dr. O'Connell specifically geared to the everyday needs of ordinary families. Future books in this series will address the challenges of making tough decisions and maintaining a personal spirituality in the face of life's constant pressures.

Timothy O'Connell welcomes the reflections of his readers. You may contact him by mail at:

> Institute of Pastoral Studies
> Loyola University Chicago
> 6525 N. Sheridan Road
> Chicago, IL 60626

You may also contact him by e-mail at:

> toconne@luc.edu